ID675930

McSWEENEY'S 43

© 2013 McSweeney's Quarterly Concern and the contributors, San Francisco, California.
INTERNS & VOLUNTEERS: Andrew Ridker, Melissa MacEwen, Sabrina Wise, Ida Yalzadeh, Kylie Byrd, Lucie Elven, Keziah Weir, Joey Nargizian, Nara Williams, Oona Haas, Hayden Bennett, Francesca McLaughlin, Aimee Burnett, Alessandra Bautista, Naoki O'Bryan, Mary Aiello, Milo Conroy, Dana Riess, Erin Cohen, Nick Bacarella, Ashley Rogers, Jami Smith, Bonnie Kim, Pilar E. Huerta, Tara Fetemi, Gretchen Schrafft, Rosanna Stevens, Yannic Dosenbach, Vanessa Martini. ALSO HELPING: Andi Mudd, Sam Riley, Rachel Khong, Em-J Staples, Ethan Nosowsky, Lauren Struck, Brian McMullen, Walter Green. WEBSITE: Chris Monks. SUPPORT: Sunra Thompson. OUTREACH: Alyson Sinclair. ART DIRECTOR: Dan McKinley. ASSOCIATE PUBLISHER: Adam Krefman. PUBLISHER: Laura Howard. COPY EDITOR: Phyllis Fong. ASSOCIATE EDITOR: Chelsea Hogue. MANAGING EDITOR: Jordan Bass. EDITOR: Dave Eggers.

Cover and interior art by Gregory Euclide. Printed in Michigan at Thomson-Shore Printers.

DEAR MCSWEENEY'S,

I'm writing to request an additional set of contributor copies of Issue 40, which contains my story "Big Windows." I don't think I'll be able to retrieve the box you previously sent, and I'm very eager to give a copy to my friend, for whom I wrote the story. It's not about her or inspired by her or dedicated to her—my writing it was an actual Christmas present, in 2009, back when we were dating. I composed it entirely on a typewriter, and typed out large portions of it more than a dozen times. By the end, I had every word of the story memorized, so she didn't even need to read it—she would just ask me to recite it to her while we lay together in bed.

The whereabouts of the initial set of contributor copies you sent is a bit of a mystery, but I strongly suspect they are in the possession of one Nogivenname Prophet, who lives in my old house on Dorgenois Street, in New Orleans. It's a half-double shotgun my roommate and I got sick of living in sometime after you requested my address. He had to walk through my bedroom to get from his room to the bathroom or kitchen, plus there were flocks of roosters running around that crowed at all hours of the day and night.

After learning from your editorial department that my books had been signed for by *NPRIFIT*, I e-mailed my old landlady to ask who lived there now. She replied: "I haven't heard anything. The new tenant is a nice man. He's Haitian but speaks reasonably good English. His name is Nogivenname (for real!) Prophet. I don't have a phone number."

I knocked on Nogivenname's door one afternoon last month. I heard noises inside, and after what seemed like a really long time, a stout middle-aged man in shorts and a T-shirt opened the door. His face was round, with a thick brow and a deep dimple on his chin, and something fine and light gray covering his cheeks that could have been stubble or ash. He propped himself up on the doorframe and clearly had a hard time moving around. The house was dark, but I could see a four-foot-tall statue that looked vaguely religious in the front room, where my roommate's bed had been, and farther back there was a table full of burning votive candles. The man did not seem happy to see me.

I explained my situation, and he said he did not have my package. His speech was slow and staggered. I told him that someone named "N. Prophet" had signed for it at this address. He looked over my shoulder, toward the horizon, and said, "I am Prophet." Upon pressing him further, he conceded that perhaps his nurse had signed for it, and said that he would check. I stood there dumbly, waiting for him.

"I'm crippled!" he nearly hollered at me. "I'll check! Don't come back here without calling!"

"Okay, okay," I begrudged, backing down the stoop. He shut the door with force.

I paused on the sidewalk, having registered that I had just promised to call a man whose phone number I did not possess. I looked back up at the blank, blue door, impotent.

I imagine he was having something of a similar moment on the other side, because he pulled the door back open moments later, his demeanor completely transformed.

"Ha ha, I'm so stupid!" he chuckled. "I don't even have your phone number!" I gave it to him, and we parted on what I perceived as good terms.

After not hearing from Prophet for five or so days, I went back. The kids next door circled around the front of the house on their bicycles, looking at me. A woman answered the door when I knocked, I'd guess in her thirties, with long, curving, tremendously decorated nails. She gave me a look I took to express a sort of what-could-you-possibly-be-doing-knocking-on-this-man's-door befuddlement. I began to explain myself, but was cut off by a shout—Prophet's—from somewhere near behind the door: "I'm sick! I'm sick!"

"He's sick," she said.

I gathered. I told her he had my number, and asked he get in touch.

Two weeks passed: nothing.

Back to Prophet's. This time, I vowed not to leave without the package or at least his phone number, and depending on how things went, without instilling Prophet with a healthy guilt trip.

But he was in good spirits. He told me he'd asked his nurse, and went on to imitate her in a high-pitched, womanish voice: "Oh, I've got all kinds of packages!" He was working on it. He gave me his phone number, which I had to memorize since I lacked paper and pen, and told me to call him after 10 a.m. the next day, adding that this was a good time because it was shortly after his daily medications.

"Can I ask you a personal question?" he said then. "What's in the package?"

"Books," I said, and began to explain the importance of the story. But he stopped me. "Books" was information enough.

The short story in question has actually become something of a dark mark. I wrote it based on an inside joke that my then-girlfriend and I had come up with one night at the grocery store, in the produce section, the precise origins of which I don't quite recall: what would happen if we woke up one morning and one of us had become mentally handicapped in the night? We riffed on this, thinking each other hilarious, until some woman turned and scowled at me after an overly loud remark I'd made involving anal sex.

My girlfriend and I kept it up over the next few weeks, reveling in our morbidity and the black humor we could squeeze from it. When I decided to write a story for her, it seemed the perfect theme with which to begin.

But after I gave her the story, which she loved, life imitated art in a pretty profoundly fucked-up way and, though both of us still have our mental capacities, something happened—I can't go into it—that resembled something that happens in the story and, in my estimation, resulted in the end of our relationship. It was an awful several months for both of us. We acknowledged the—incidental, eerie—closeness of our situation to the story's plot, and then we split despite my asking her to marry me, twice. We've only recently begun to become real friends again, and it will mean a lot for me to give her a copy of the journal with her story in it, signed. I had dinner with her the other night for the first time in more than a year, and it wasn't as painful or awkward as it has been, but I had sort of scheduled our meeting around having the gift to give her, and its absence was felt.

Anyway, I called Prophet at the agreed-upon time the next day. "Hey, Prophet," I chimed, like we were old friends. "It's Nate." He said his nurse had told him she had put several packages in a drawer, and that he would check his drawers and call me right back—which, I wasn't surprised, he didn't. I called the next day and left a message. I called the morning two days after that, and didn't leave a message.

I was lying in bed the day after that, still bleary-eyed from my birthday party, which had taken place the night before. Before I got up

I received a call from a local number neither I nor my telephone recognized. I answered, but no one spoke directly back. I could hear several voices, one of them distinctly Prophet's; it sounded like they were arguing, or like the television was on, or maybe like Prophet was arguing with the television. In any case, there was a sense of urgency on the other end of the line, but I couldn't make out the words. They blurred into my ear as wavering pitches, volumes, and inflections, human and alien at the same time. I tried to imagine what was taking place in my old house— Prophet told me he rarely leaves—whether my package was sitting in a drawer among the voices, whether Prophet was all right or suffering. I listened for a long time, occasionally saying "Hello?", my head resting on my pillow. Then I hung up.

Yours,

NATHAN C. MARTIN
NEW ORLEANS, LA

PS I still haven't received my check. Please send to my current address.

DEAR MCSWEENEY'S,

My cousin is in her first year at Harvard Medical School, and my mother raised me, so you can imagine how much weight their advice carries. Recently they both mentioned, independent of each other, that I should get a physical. Both were disappointed that I couldn't remember when I'd last had one. My guess was I'd gone before I started college; otherwise I wouldn't have been allowed to move into the dorms, right?

I ended up looking online for providers, and found one so close to my house that I would most likely not be late to my appointment. That's how I chose my doctor. It's probably my fault the visit was a chemical fire.

When I called to set up a visit, I was informed that, as a new patient, there would be no physical exam during the initial appointment. It would only be a meet and greet; the doctor and I would be there to establish our relationship.

Weirdly refreshing, I murmured to myself. What a throwback to a simpler, less extortionist time! I've heard so much about how impersonal doctor visits are these days; I had been prepared for the cold, five-minute in and out. Somehow, it seemed, my search engine had scuttled past everything that is wrong with our health care system.

Appointment day arrived. The doctor came in upbeat and very engaged, tricking me. She patted my knee as she walked by—which I appreciated, but now see as a harbinger of the death of the Hippocratic oath. She looked at me so avidly my eyes gradually wandered to the floor.

"So, how did you hear about me?" she said.

Her face was expectant, poised to (I'm pretty sure) receive notice of glowing referrals. I readjusted my position in my chair.

"Uh, the provider list," I said. "This office is really close to my house."

She nodded in swift hiccups. She said, "So none of your friends go to me?" Her face was still open, but straining. At this point I was compelled to manage her feelings, because sometimes I am very compassionate.

I said, "Well, they definitely could, but we don't really talk about our doctors."

I couldn't tell if this made her feel better, but she moved on.

She asked, "So do you need an STD screening?"

"No, I'm good on all that, thanks," I said. "Just went to the gynecologist last month."

She looked down at her clipboard. "Okay, but, just so you know, I do all that stuff. It's my field. I mean, I teach at universities, I'm on panels. It's kind of my thing."

"Oh," I said. "That's great."

"Yeah, it's definitely my thing. You could come to me with any questions, or tests you need done... So who's your gyno?"

"You know," I said. "I can't quite remember the name. They were on the provider list."

"Okay. Well, you can do all that with me from now on. I'm, you know, you can come to me. I do it all."

"Okay," I said, "sure, yes. Streamlining. Sure." Faint alarms buzzed in my mind.

But I am naive and a pleaser, so I stayed supportive of her and second-guessed myself. I couldn't remember what it was like to see a general practitioner. Maybe they always tried to be your gynecologist, as well?

She skimmed the forms I had filled out. "Well, you seem very healthy," she said. "You're in a relationship? That lowers your risk factors." She looked at me a long while. Instinctively, I started to squirm. "Well. Now I'm looking at your face. What's that, that blemish? Does that happen when you get your period?"

"Yes, sometimes," I said, trying to hide my chin from her.

"Have you ever been on birth control?"

"What? Um, yes."

"But you're not now?"

"Well, I had weird reactions to it. And—"

"You should get on birth control. It will regulate your hormones."

"Riiiiight," I said, truly confused now. "But... I'm sorry, what are we talking about?"

"Everything is a matter of hormones," she said. "They just need to be regulated."

"Okay, yes, but I think I'm doing an okay job on my own." I tried a slow smile to show that I was open to suggestions, yet incredibly self-assured.

"Do you cramp a lot on your period?"

"No, I don't," I said. The alarms were getting louder.

"Well, on birth control you would cramp even less. You could get the ring; you could go all year without having a period. There is no [here she made finger quotation marks] 'need to bleed.' As a matter of fact, as recently as two hundred years ago, you would spend years and years not bleeding, because you would be pregnant the entire time."

I wanted the tiny hammer on my kneecaps; I wanted to see a stethoscope. I did not want to hear any more talk about the bleeding of frontier women.

But she was still talking.

"There are things we inherit, no use questioning it. Me, I'm fifty years old and I have not one gray hair on my head. Because of my father. You, you're almost thirty, and look." She pointed to my chin. "That's probably because of your parents. It's all hormones. So, you want to leave here with a prescription?"

At that instant I had a fantasy: I was meeting her for the first time at a dinner party, learning what she did for a living, absorbing her personality, and then walking away, forever, grateful she wasn't my doctor.

"No, thank you," I said. "I'm okay for now."

She was looking at what I assume was a checklist. "Have you ever had depression?"

"No," I lied.

"Both your parents healthy?"

"Yes, I guess."

"You see both your parents?"

"Um, just my mom, mostly."

"What happened to your dad?"

"My dad? He and I don't talk that much."

"Are you in therapy?"

I panicked. I had to derail her. I asked, "What about skin cancer? Can you check me for skin cancer? I know this isn't the exam part, but my cousin said I should get my moles checked for skin cancer."

"Okay, well, sure, I can check," she said. "Do you have moles you want me to look at?"

I scanned my arms and legs for anything. "No, but maybe on my back? I can't see my back."

She told me to get on the exam table. She started checking my back. I thought, This feels more normal. Now she was acting like a doctor. In my mind I chanted: *Shhh, shhh, don't talk, don't talk.*

"All clear!" she said. "No moles."

I was putting my shirt back on, brainstorming something to mumble as I fled.

"Well," she was saying, "I know this might not come up for you, but just so you know…"

My breath caught. I couldn't possibly know.

"I do abortions. Right here, in this office. You could get one here, if you ever needed to."

I made a long humming noise and tapped my right thumb, which is what I do when a doctor tries to sell me a future abortion.

"I'm very active with reproductive rights. I've served on a lot of panels. I've written about it, I teach. I'm really strong in the field. You should come to me, if you ever, you know."

I sat on the edge of the exam table, legs swinging.

"I mean, you never know what could happen. You said you tour, right? So. I'm here. And your friends, you could let them know, too."

I nodded once, exhaled. Yes, I could.

She smiled at me. "Just in case. I'll be here." She stood and took my hand. "It was so great to meet you."

She walked me out and asked the receptionist to schedule me for the physical. I tried to tell the receptionist "NO!" with my eyes, but nothing transmitted. I canceled the next day.

Now I have a different doctor. And yes, they're in the same office. I know, I know. It's just… They're so close to my house.

THAO NGUYEN
SAN FRANCISCO, CA

DEAR MCSWEENEY'S,

Sometimes when I'm blue, I like to imagine a man trying to teach long division to a duck. "Write the remainder up there, duck," he says. "Duck. The remainder goes up there." His wife, from their bedroom, calls down, "Honey, the duck can't hold a pen. Come to bed."

"Can't hold a pen *yet*," the man mutters. He sits in silence for a long time. The duck pecks at a little piece of a cracker.

How do you deal with the blues?

Sincerely,

AVERY MONSEN
QUEENS, NY

DEAR MCSWEENEY'S,

I have a very nice sweater that I bought at the Gap a couple years ago. It's not particularly flashy or anything—just a green zippered cardigan—but for some reason it gets more compliments than any other piece of clothing I own.

"That's a nice sweater," a stranger will tell me. "Where'd you get it?"

"The Gap."

Everyone's reaction to this is the same, and it strikes so quickly that they can't hide it: crushing disappointment. They get angry at themselves, and I can almost hear the internal dialogue. *Why'd I think that was such a great sweater? It's just some dumb, normal Gap sweater.* They really beat themselves up over it. *I thought I had a more discerning eye!*

This seems crazy, but I guess if you care enough to say, "Nice sweater," you're the type of person who takes knitwear seriously. I'm a big cheese fan, and I remember keenly the embarrassment I once felt at a wine tasting when I thought I was eating brie and discovered it was actually a napkin.

However, this is only the first stage of their disappointment. After their initial shock, they invariably turn their anger outward—toward me, the hobo who has scammed a compliment out of them. *Why doesn't this hick shop at fancier stores?* they think. They'll narrow their eyes, scrutinizing my shabby loafers. *I can see now he's a laborer, but that doesn't mean he couldn't save a couple weeks' wages and splurge on something at Barneys.* They begin to wonder if I even bought the sweater at the Gap. Wasn't it more likely that I stole it? Perhaps it looked familiar because they had seen it on the news...

I could lie and say I bought the sweater in Milan, but I don't want to. I'm surprised people find the Gap so scandalously low-class, and it's making me doubt my own sanity. There's a clothing store called the Gap, isn't there? It's not actually a chain of strip clubs, or a carpet-remnant store I don't know about?

I shouldn't have to lie about my sweater.

Unashamed,

DOOGIE HORNER

PHILADELPHIA, PA

DEAR MCSWEENEY'S,

Back on November 6, I voted for Proposition 34 to repeal the death penalty here in California. It was effectively a vote to end my job, but I still voted Yes.

I'm a specialized private investigator, a "mitigation specialist." Defense attorneys hire me to research and document the life histories of their clients—men (and they are almost always men) who are facing the death penalty. I seek out material for the attorneys to use, either when imploring juries for mercy or when appealing to State Supreme Court justices to convert a trial court's death sentence to life in prison without the possibility of parole. It's difficult and sad work, but it's often rewarding and interesting. It also pays pretty well.

Yet I would have been happy to say good-bye to it. Despite decades of U.S. Supreme Court decisions to ensure the death penalty would not be a "cruel and unusual punishment," it remains exactly so. And since the penalty was reintroduced in California in 1978, it's been sucking billions of dollars out of the state's coffers. That's why I, and others like me whose incomes are similarly tied to the state's "machinery of death," woke up on November 6 hoping for a Yes on Prop 34 victory.

But Prop 34 lost. I've still got my job, and over seven hundred condemned men (there are nineteen condemned women in the state, as well, housed at Chowchilla) remain on California's death row. Inside the 150-year-old San Quentin State Prison, which overlooks part of the beautiful San Francisco Bay, these men will continue to live their double punishment: prolonged incarceration under terrible psychological and physical conditions, all the while awaiting execution.

Prop 34 was intended to replace execution with Life without the Possibility of Parole (LWOP). The convicted would suffer no death sentence, just those same terrible psychological and physical conditions for the rest of their lives. To know something of those conditions is to suspect that at least some of the prisoners doing LWOP would have viewed a Prop 34 victory as simply replacing one harsh sentence with another, equally harsh punishment. It's "the second death sentence," as an LWOP prisoner called it in a 2004 essay in a local Bay Area paper.

Perhaps Prop 34 failed precisely because voters were blind to the real meaning of an LWOP sentence. Perhaps those "No" voters held views similar to the *New York Times* reader who, back in September 2011, wrote a letter to the editor complaining that LWOP was not a "suitable punishment of heinous crimes" because, in "today's prisons, inmates participate in sports activities and have access to libraries, entertainment and medical care."

How wrong that reader was. Today's prisons are not just facilities that suspend your liberty, a catastrophic and traumatic event in itself; they are also dangerous and horrific places. LWOP condemns the prisoner to a lifetime of daily threats of violence from other prisoners or prison workers, inadequate and innutritious food, frequent humiliations, long stretches of debilitating idleness, arbitrary restrictions and punishments, and the mayhem of overcrowded facilities.

LWOP is a life spent

with the constant tension of avoiding any appearance of weakness, so as to not invite intimidation and aggression. Everything that, to a free person, looks marginally bearable about prison life has a violent flip side. Exercise yards, for example, are also stabbing grounds. Watching and interpreting the movements of other prisoners is a crucial skill, as is learning which guards might suddenly decide to make your life miserable. There are few inmates who have not listened, grimly, as a prisoner was beaten by a guard, or seen a stabbed and dying prisoner dragged off an exercise yard, or stepped over the pool of blood and vomit left on a tier by a violent encounter.

A sentence of LWOP means that you will never be free from the threat of terror. According to David Kaiser and Lovisa Stannow in their recent *New York Review of Books* piece on prison rape, a Bureau of Justice Statistics study found "approximately one in ten former state prisoners were sexually abused while serving their most recent sentences." And half of all sexual abuse in detention is committed by staff, not by inmates. There is no safe place in prison.

Then there's the principal method of individual control: solitary confinement. If there is a way for prisons to make LWOP even more excruciating, it is this. The core of solitary is social isolation combined with sensory deprivation. A former client of mine spends most of his time in a concrete and steel cell whose door connects first to a vestibule big enough to fit a human being before reaching another door, which opens into a corridor. He cannot hear or see people passing by. Food is slid to him on a tray through a slot in the nearest door. Books and writing materials are controlled. He showers in his cell, and when he does get to exercise he does it on his own, inside a large concrete box where the only view is up to the sky. He landed in solitary because of violence committed within the prison walls; the story was that he killed another inmate, which was his only alternative to being killed himself. Keep in mind that there was no court case establishing this, or any witness that we could find who saw any violence from our client when he was on the outside. He was a lousy meth dealer who got a huge sentence and had to make prison his home.

LWOP is living the burden of a life devoid of forgiveness and without hope. Another LWOP inmate recently wrote to me after learning that all his appeals against the sentence had failed. "I can't do life without a chance of ever getting out," he said. "Prison just eats at you and it never gets any better, just worser and worser. All your friends and family forget about you and then the loneliness eats you."

Capital case defense teams try to not let the thought of LWOP disturb them. A jury's LWOP verdict over death is a victory. I still hold this to be true, but as I write this letter I recall our last "victory." He's wearing an orange jumpsuit, and he's standing on the right side of the courtroom, just in front of the door that leads to the holding cells. The judge has handed down the sentence and wished him good luck. The sheriff's deputy is taking hold of him by the upper arm, and he's turning in that awkward manner that signals shackled feet. But as he turns, he briefly glances into the public gallery to catch a glimpse of whomever may be there for him. There's no family member, but there is a mother of an old girlfriend who had, years earlier, witnessed his potential for a different path, and who understood how it was lost to poverty, alcoholism, neglect, and mental instability. She had wanted our client to accept some responsibility for the destructive parts of his life, but she, like his legal team, had come to appreciate how deep his frailties were. Now, with a quick nod to his ex's mom, he's ushered through the courtroom's well-varnished door, and disappears from us and from the free world for the rest of his life.

RACHEL SOMMERVILLE
ALBANY, CA

DEAR MCSWEENEY'S,

Outside of wedging the moving truck into a Chicago alley, neglecting to lock a bathroom door at a McDonald's, and hitting a bird in close proximity to the Carter Center for Peace, the move to Atlanta was great. My wife's job has placed us here in Georgia for one year, and we're trying to maximize the experience. We have drunk beers in a graveyard with history buffs; we've listened to jazz played by a fantastic family band aboard an indoor ship captained by a Renaissance man named Dante; we have found a great church, truly Catholic, where parishioners from more than sixty countries celebrate Mass just down the road from an old prominent Klan meeting place. And the local football team won a record number of games, allowing my wife and I, thanks to a Papa John's promotion, to consume a record number of pizzas, half-price.

We do have loud neighbors, though. They scream and holler frequently about cars and locked doors and money. The man chops wood in his front yard regularly, often between deep night and early morning. They have barking dogs, too, and a piebald cat that they let roam the streets. It is a friendly cat, an amazing cat. Everyone who comes through the neighborhood dotes on it. It runs up to all, stranger or familiar, human or dog, and emits full love.

The "Dammit"s and "Fucking Door"s shouted by our neighbors are easy to decipher through our thin walls, but the name they call the cat is not. We think it's Jukebox, and call it such.

Now, I've never thought myself a catnapper, nor committed such acts as to justify the label. But I'm just curious, *McSweeney's*, as the closest thing I have to a lawyer—what kind of time would I be looking at if I happen to keep this cat for myself when we move? And if the matter were to be settled out of court, *McSweeney's*, as the closest thing I have to a doctor, how life-threatening are ax blows?

Sincerely,

PATRICK SHAFFNER
ATLANTA, GA

CHARITY

by CHARLES BAXTER

1

He had fallen into bad trouble. He had worked in Ethiopia for a year—teaching in a school and lending a hand at a medical clinic. He had eaten all the local foods and been stung by the many airborne insects. When he'd returned to the States, he'd brought back an infection—the inflammation in his knees and his back and his shoulders was so bad that sometimes he could hardly stand up. Probably a viral arthritis, his doctor said. It happens. Here: have some painkillers.

Borrowing a car, he drove down from Minneapolis to the Mayo Clinic, where after two days of tests the doctors

informed him that they would have no firm diagnosis for
the next month or so. Back in Minneapolis, through a
friend of a friend, he visited a wildcat homeopathy treat-
ment center known for traumatic-pain-relief treatments.
The center, in a strip mall storefront claiming to be a
weight loss clinic (WEIGHT NO MORE), gave him megadoses
of meadowsweet, a compound chemically related to aspirin.
After two months without health insurance or prescription
coverage, he had emptied his bank account, and he gazed at
the future with shy dread.

Through another friend of a friend, he managed to
get his hands on a few superb prescription painkillers, the
big ones, gifts from heaven. With the aid of these pills, he
felt like himself again. He blessed his own life. He cooked
some decent meals; he called his boyfriend in Seattle; he
went around town looking for a job; he made plans to get
himself to the Pacific Northwest. When the drugs ran out
and the pain returned, worse this time, like being stabbed
in his elbows and shoulders, along with the novelty of
addiction's chills and fevers, the friend-of-a-friend told him
that if he wanted more pills at the going street rate, he
had better go see Black Bird. He could find Black Bird at
the bar of a club, The Inner Circle, on Hennepin Avenue.
"He's always there," the friend-of-a-friend said. "He's there
now. He reads. The guy sits there studying Shakespeare.
Used to be a scholar or something. Pretends to be a Native
American, one of those imposter types. Very easy to spot.
I'll tell him you're coming."

The next Wednesday, he found Black Bird at the end of
the Inner Circle bar near the broken jukebox and the sign
for the men's room. The club's walls had been built from
limestone and rust-red brick and sported no decorative

motifs of any kind. If you needed decorations around you when you drank, you went somewhere else. The peculiar orange lighting was so dim that Quinn couldn't figure out how Black Bird could read at all.

Quinn approached him gingerly. Black Bird's hair went down to his shoulders. The gray in it looked as if it had been applied with chalk. He wore bifocals and moved his finger down the page as he read. Nearby was a half-consumed bottle of 7Up.

"Excuse me. Are you Black Bird?"

Without looking up, the man said, "Why do you ask?"

"I'm Quinn." He held out his hand. Black Bird did not take it. "My friend Morrow told me about you."

"Ah huh," Black Bird said. He glanced up with an impatient expression before returning to his book. Quinn examined the text. Black Bird was reading *Othello*, the third act.

"Morrow said I should come see you. There's something I need."

Black Bird said nothing.

"I need it pretty bad," Quinn said, his hand trembling inside his pocket. He wasn't used to talking to people like this. When Black Bird didn't respond, Quinn said, "You're reading *Othello*." Quinn had acquired a liberal arts degree from a college in Iowa, where he had majored in global political solutions, and he felt that he had to assert himself. "The handkerchief. And Iago, right?"

Black Bird nodded. "This isn't College Bowl," he said dismissively. With his finger stopped on the page, he said, "What do you want from me?"

Quinn whispered the name of the drug that made him feel human.

"What a surprise," said Black Bird. "Well, well. How do I know that you're not a cop? You a cop, Mr. Quinn?"

"No."

"Because I don't know what you're asking me or what you're talking about. I'm a peaceful man sitting here reading this book and drinking this 7Up."

"Yes," Quinn said.

"You could always come back in four days," Black Bird said. "You could always bring some money." He mentioned a price for a certain number of painkillers. "I have to get the ducks in a row."

"That's a lot of cash," Quinn said. Then, after thinking it over, he said, "All right." He did not feel that he had many options these days.

Black Bird looked up at him with an expression devoid of interest or curiosity.

"Do you read, Mr. Quinn?" he asked. "Everybody should read something. Otherwise we all fall down into the pit of ignorance. Many are down there. Some people fall in it forever. Their lives mean nothing. They should not exist." Black Bird spoke these words in a bland monotone.

"I don't know what to read," Quinn told him, his legs shaking.

"Too bad," Black Bird said. "Next time you come here, bring a book. I need proof you exist. The Minneapolis Public Library is two blocks away. But if you come back, bring the money. Otherwise, there's no show."

Quinn was living very temporarily in a friend's basement in Northeast Minneapolis. His parents, in a traditional old-world gesture, had disowned him after he had come out, so he couldn't call on them for support. They had uttered several unforgettable verdicts about his character, sworn they would never see him again, and that was that.

He had a sister who lived in Des Moines with her husband and two children. She did not like what she called Quinn's "sexual preferences" and had a tendency to hang up on him. None of his friends from high school had any money he could borrow. The acquaintance in whose basement he was staying was behind on his rent. His student debt had been taken up by a collection agency, which was calling him three times a day.

Quinn's boyfriend in Seattle, a field rep for a medical supply company, had a thing about people borrowing money. He might break up with Quinn if Quinn asked him for a loan. He could be prickly, the boyfriend, and the two of them were still on a trial basis anyway. They had met in Africa and had fallen in love over there. The love might not travel if Quinn brought up the subject of debts or his viral arthritis and inflammation or the drug habit he had recently acquired.

Now that the painkillers had run out, a kind of groggy unfocused physical discomfort had become Quinn's companion day and night. He lived in the house that the pain had designed for him. The Mayo Clinic had not called him back, and the meadowsweet's effect was like a cup of water dropped on a house fire. Sometimes the pain started in Quinn's knees and circled around Quinn's back until it located itself in his shoulders, like exploratory surgery performed using a Swiss Army Knife. He had acquired the jitters and a runny nose and a swollen tongue and cramps. He couldn't sleep and had diarrhea. He was a mess, and the knowledge of the mess he had become made the mess worse. The necessity of opiates became a supreme idea that forced out all the other ideas until only one thought occupied Quinn's mind: *Get those painkillers*. He didn't think he was a goner yet, though.

He could no longer tell his dreams from his waking life. The things around him began to take on the appearance of stage props made from cardboard. Other people—pedestrians—looked like shadow creatures giving off a stinky perfume.

In the basement room where he slept, there was, leaning against the wall, a baseball bat, a Louisville Slugger, and one night after dark, in a dreamlike hallucinatory fever, he took it across the Hennepin Avenue Bridge to a park along the Mississippi, where he hid hotly shivering behind a tree until the right sort of prosperous person walked by. Quinn felt as if he were under orders to do what he was about to do. The man he chose wore a T-shirt and jeans and seemed fit but not so strong as to be dangerous, and after rushing out from the shadows, Quinn hit him with the baseball bat in the back of his legs. He had aimed for the back of the legs so he wouldn't shatter the guy's kneecaps. When Quinn's victim fell down, Quinn reached into the man's trouser pocket and pulled out his wallet and ran away with it, dropping the Slugger into the river as he crossed the bridge.

Back in his friend's basement, Quinn examined the wallet's contents. His hands were trembling again, and he couldn't see properly, and he wasn't sure he was awake, but he could make out that the name on the driver's license was Benjamin Takemitsu. The man didn't look Japanese in the driver's license photo, but Quinn didn't think much about it until he'd finished counting the cash, which amounted to $321, an adequate sum for a few days' relief. At that point he gazed more closely at the photo and saw that Takemitsu appeared to be intelligently thoughtful. What had he done to this man? Familiar pain flared behind Quinn's knees and in his neck, punishment he recognized that he deserved, and the pain pushed out everything else.

He called his boyfriend in Seattle. In a panic he told him that he had robbed someone named Benny Takemitsu, that he had used a baseball bat. The boyfriend said, "You've had a bad dream, Matty. That didn't happen. You would never do such a thing. Go back to sleep, sweetheart, and I'll call you tomorrow."

After that he lay awake wondering what had become of the person he had once been, the one who had gone to Africa. To the ceiling, he said, "I am no longer myself." He did not know who this new person was, the man whom he had become, but when he finally fell asleep, he saw in his dream one of those shabby castoffs with whom you wouldn't want to have any encounters, any business at all, someone who belonged on the sidewalk with a cardboard sign that read HELP ME. The man was crouched behind a tree in the dark, peering out with feverish eyes. His own face was the face of the castoff.

Somehow he would have to make it up to Benny Takemitsu.

In The Inner Circle, when Quinn entered, Black Bird did not look up. He was seated in his usual place, and once again his finger was traveling down the page. *Cymbeline*, this time, a play that Quinn had never read.

"It's you," Black Bird said.

"Yes," Quinn said.

"Did you bring a book of your own?"

"No."

"All right," Black Bird said. "I can't say I'm surprised."

He then issued elaborate instructions to Quinn about where in the men's room to put the money, and when he, Black Bird, would retrieve it. The entire exchange took over half an hour, though the procedure hardly seemed secret or designed to fool anyone. When Quinn finally returned to his basement room, he had already gulped down two of the pills, and his relief soon grew to a great size. He felt his humanity restored until his mottled face appeared before him in the bathroom mirror, and then he realized belatedly what terrible trouble he was in.

Two days later he disappeared.

2

That was as far as I got whenever I tried to compose an account of what happened to Matty Quinn—my boyfriend, my soulmate, my future life—the man who mistakenly thought I was a tightwad. I *was* very thrifty in Ethiopia, convinced that Americans should not spend large sums in front of people who owned next to nothing. But to Matty I would have given anything. Upon his return to Minneapolis he had called me up and texted and e-mailed me with these small clues about the medical ordeal he was going through, and I had not understood; then he had called to say that he had robbed this Takemitsu, and I had not believed him. Then he disappeared from the world, from his existence and mine.

Two weeks later the investigating officer in the Minneapolis Police Department (whom I had contacted in my desperation) told me that I could certainly come to survey the city if I wished to. After all, this Officer Erickson said, nothing is stopping you from trying to find your friend, although I understand that your permanent home is in Seattle and you do not know anyone here. It's a free country, so you're welcome to try. However, circumstances being what they are, I wouldn't get your hopes up if I were you. The odds are against it. People go missing, he said. Addicts especially. The street absorbs them. Your friend might be living in a ditch.

He did not say these words with the distancing sarcasm or condescension that straight men sometimes use on queers. He simply sounded bored and hopeless.

Matthew Quinn. First he was Matt. Then he was Matty. These two syllables formed on my tongue as I spoke his name repeatedly into his ear and then into his mouth. That was before he was gone.

This is how we'd met: I had come by the clinic, the one where he worked, to deliver some medical supplies from the company I was then working for, and I saw him near a window whose slatted light fell across the face of a feverish young woman who lay on a bed under mosquito netting. She was resting quietly with her eyes closed and her hand rising to her forehead in an almost unconscious gesture. She was very thin. You could see it in her skinny veined forearms and her prominent cheekbones. On one cheekbone was a J-shaped scar.

Close by, a boy about nine years old sat on a chair watching her. I had the impression that they had both been there, mother and son, for a week or so. Four other patients immobilized by illness were in other beds scattered around the room. Outside a dog barked in the local language, Amharic, and the air inside remained motionless except for some random agitation under a rattling ceiling fan. The hour was just past midday, and very hot.

That's when I noticed Quinn: he was approaching the woman with a cup in his hand, and after getting himself underneath the mosquito netting, he supported her head as he helped her drink the water, or medicine (I couldn't see what it was), in the cup. Then he turned and, still under the mosquito netting, spoke to the boy in Amharic. His Amharic was better than mine, but I could understand it. He was saying that the boy's mother would be all right but that her recovery would take some time.

The boy nodded.

It was a small, simple gesture of kindness, his remembering to speak to that child. Not everybody would go to the effort. Even when the woman's husband arrived— sweaty, gesticulating, his eyes narrowed with irritation and fear—to complain about the conditions, Quinn smiled, sat him down, and calmed him. Soon the three of them were speaking softly, so that I could not hear what they said.

Young white Americans come to Africa all the time, some to make money, as I did, others in the grip of mostly harmless youthful idealistic delusions. Much of the time, they are operating out of the purest post-colonial sentimentality. I was there on business, for which I don't apologize. But when I saw that this man, Matty Quinn, was indeed doing good works without any hope of reward, it touched me. Compassion was an unthinking habit with him. He was kind by nature, without anyone asking him to be.

Sometimes you arrive at love before going through the first stage of attraction. The light from the window illuminated his body as he helped that sick woman and then squatted down to speak to the boy and his father. After that I found myself imprinted with his face; it gazed at me in daydreams. Here it is, or was: slightly narrow, with hooded eyes and thick eyebrows over modestly stubbled cheeks, and sensual lips from which that day came words of solace so tender-hearted that I thought: *This isn't natural; he must be queer*. And indeed he was, as I found out a week later, sitting with him in a café over cups of the local mudlike coffee. He didn't realize how his kindness and his charity had pierced me until I told him about my own vulnerabilities, and the erotic directions in which I was inclined, whereupon he looked at me with an expression of amused relief. When I confessed how the sight of him had stunned me, he said, very thoughtfully, "I can help you with that," and then he put his hand on my knee so quickly that even I hardly noticed the gesture.

Being white and gay in Ethiopia is no easy matter, but we managed it by meeting on weekends in the nearest city. We'd go to multinational hotels, the impersonal expense-account Hiltons with which I am familiar and where they don't care who you are. In those days, before he got sick, Matty Quinn walked around with a lilt, his arm half-raised in a potential greeting, as if he were seeking voters. His good humor and sense made his happiness contagious. A good soul has a certain lightness and lifts up those who surround it. He lifted me. We fucked like champions and then poured wine for each other. I loved him for himself and for how he made me feel. I wonder if Jesus had that effect on people. I think so.

By the time we both came back to the States, however, Quinn was already sick. I said I could fly out to see him, but he asked me not to, given his present condition. He was living in a friend's basement, he told me, and was looking around for a job, and he didn't want me to visit until his circumstances had improved. That was untrue, about the job. Instead, he was losing himself. He was breaking down. He was particulating. When he disappeared, I resolved to find him.

Entering The Lower Depths, the bar on Hennepin that I finally identified as the place that Quinn had described to me, I saw, through the tumult of louts near the entryway, a man sitting at the back of the bar, reading a book. He did not have graying black hair, but he did wear glasses, so I made my way toward him, reflexively curling my fingers into fists. I elbowed into a nearby space and ordered a beer. After waiting for a lull in the background noise and finding none, I shouted, "What's that you're reading?"

"Shakespeare!"

"Which play?"

"Not a play! The sonnets."

"Well, I'll be! When in disgrace with fortune and men's eyes!" I quoted loudly, with a calculating, companionable smile on my face. I extended my hand. "Name's Albert. Harry Albert."

The man nodded but did not extend his hand in return. "Two first names? Well, I'm Blackburn."

"Black Bird?"

"No. Blackburn. Horace *Blackburn*."

"Right. My friend told me about you!"

"Who's your friend?"

"Matt Quinn."

Blackburn shook his head. "Don't know him."

"Okay, you don't know him. But do you know where I might find him?"

"How could I know where he is if I don't know him?"

"Just a suspicion!" Doing business in central Africa, I had gotten used to wily characters; I was accustomed to their smug expressions of guarded cunning. They always gave themselves away by their self-amused trickster smirks. I had learned to keep pressing on these characters until they just got irritated with me.

"Come on, Mr. Blackburn," I said. "Let's not pretend. Let's get in the game here and then go to the moon, all right?"

"I don't know where he is," Blackburn insisted. I wondered how long this clown had carried on as a pseudo-Indian peddling narcotic painkillers to lowlife addicts and to upstanding citizens who then became addicts. Probably for years, maybe since childhood. And the Shakespeare! Just a bogus literary affectation. He smelled of breath mints and had a tattoo on his neck.

"However," he said slyly, "if I *were* looking for him, I'd go down to the river and I'd search for him in the shadows by the Hennepin Avenue Bridge." Blackburn then displayed an unwitting smile. "Guys like that turn into trolls, you know?" His eyes flashed. "Faggot trolls especially."

Reaching over with profound deliberation, I spilled the man's 7Up over his edition of Shakespeare, dropped some money on the bar, and walked out. If this unregistered barroom brave wanted to follow me, I was ready. Every man should know how to throw a good punch, gay men especially. I have a remarkably quick combination of left jabs and a right uppercut, and I can take a punch without crumpling. Mine is not a glass jaw. You hit me, you hit a stone.

Outside the bar, I asked a policeman to point me in the direction of the Mississippi River, which he did with a bored, hostile stare.

I searched down there that night for Quinn, and the next night I searched for him again. For a week, I patrolled the riverbank, watching the barges pass, observing the joggers and inhaling the pleasantly fetid river air. I kept his face before me as lovers do, as a light to guide me, and like any lover I was single-minded. I spoke his name in prayer. Gradually I widened the arc of my survey to include the areas around the university and the hospitals. Many dubious characters presented themselves to me, but I am a fighter and did not fear them.

One night around one a.m., I was walking through one of the darkest sections along the river, shadowed even during the day by canopies of maple trees, when I saw in the deep obscurity a solitary man sitting on a park bench. He was barely discernible there, hardly a man at all, he had grown so thin. I could make him out from the pinpoint reflected light from buildings on the other bank.

Approaching him, I saw that this wreck was my beloved Matty Quinn, or what remained of him. I called his name. He turned his head toward me, and gave me a look of recognition colored over with indifference. He did not rise to greet me, so I could not hug him. He emanated an odor of the river, as if he had been living in it. After I sat down next to him, I tenderly took him into my arms

as if he would break. But he had already been broken.
I kissed his cheek. Something terrible had happened to
him, but he recognized me; he knew me.

"I was afraid it was you, Harry," he said. "I was afraid
you would find me."

"Of course I would find you. I went searching."

He lifted up his head as if listening for something. "Do
you think we're all being watched? Do you think anything
is watching us?"

At first I thought he meant surveillance cameras, and
then I understood that he was referring to the gods. "No,"
I said. "Nothing is ever watching us, Matty. We're all
unwatched." Then I said, "I want you to come back with
me. I have a hotel room. Let me feed you and clean you up
and clothe you. I should never have left you alone, god-
damn it. I shouldn't have let you end up back here. Come
with me. Look at you. You're shivering."

"This is very sweet of you," he said. "You're admira-
ble. But the thing is, I keep waiting for him." He did not
elaborate.

"Who?"

"I keep waiting for that boy. Remember? That mother's
boy? And then when he shows up, I always hit him with a
baseball bat." This was pure dissociation.

"You're not making any sense," I said. "Let's go. Let's
get you in the shower and wash you down and order a big
steak from room service."

"No, he's *coming*," he insisted. "He'll be here any minute." And then, out of nowhere, he said, "I love you, but
I'm not here now. And I won't be. Harry, give it up. Let's
say good-bye."

I'm a businessman, very goal- and task-oriented, and

CHARLES BAXTER

I won't stand for talk like that. "Come on," I said. "Matty.
Enough of this shit. Let's go. Let's get out of here." I stood
before him and raised him by his shoulders as if he were a
huge rag doll, and together, with my arm supporting him,
we walked along the river road until by some miracle a taxi
approached us. I hailed it, and the man drove us back to
my hotel. In the lobby, the sight we presented—of a successful well-groomed gentleman holding up a shambling,
smelly wreck—raised an eyebrow at the check-in desk
from the night clerk, but eyebrows have never inflicted a
moment of pain on me.

I bathed him that night, and I shaved him, and
I ordered a cheeseburger from room service, from which
he ate two bites fed from my hand to his mouth. I put
him to bed in clean sheets, and all night he jabbered and
shivered and cried out and tried to fight me and to escape.
He actually thought he could defeat me physically, that's
how deluded he was. The next day, after a few phone calls,
I checked him into a rehab facility—they are everywhere in
this region, and he was quite willing to go—and I promised to return in ten days for a visit. They don't want you
sooner than that.

Matty Quinn was right: he was now a different
man, his soul ruined by his dealings with Black Bird, or
Blackburn, or whatever that scholar of Shakespeare was
calling himself these days, and I did not love him anymore.
I felt fairly certain that I had gone through a one-way gate
and would not be able to love him again. I can be fickle,
I admit. Yet I would not abandon him until he was ready
for it. In the meantime, out of the love I had once felt for
him, and which it had been my honor to possess, I resolved
to kill his enabler.

*　　*　　*

The next night I lured Black Bird outside The Lower Depths. I informed him that I had brought with me a bulging packet of cash, and that I would give it to him for the sake of my friend Quinn's painkilling drugs. But the cash was outside, I said, and only I could show him where. I did my best to look like a sucker.

Once in the shadows, I worked quickly and efficiently on him, and then after some minutes I left Black Bird battered on the brick pavement out of sight of the bar's alley entryway. The man was a drug dealer, and I had administered to him the beating I thought he deserved. I would have beaten Matty's doctor too, the one who first prescribed the painkillers, but they don't let you do that; you can't assault our medical professionals. Black Bird had gotten the brunt of it. But the angel of justice calls for retribution in kind, and since Matty Quinn was still alive, so, in his way, was Black Bird.

When Matty was ready to be discharged, I returned to Minneapolis and picked him up. Imagine this: the sun was blazing, and in broad daylight the man I had once loved folded himself up into my slate-gray rental car, and we drove like any old couple to the basement where he had been staying. We picked up his worldly possessions, the ones he wished to keep and to take with him to Seattle. Remnants: a high school yearbook, photographs of the village where he had worked in Ethiopia, a pair of cuff links, a clock radio, a laptop computer, a few books, and clothes, including a dark blue ascot. Not loving him, I helped him pack, and, not loving him, I bought him a ticket back to Seattle.

Saying very little, we sat together on the plane, touching hands occasionally. Not loving him, I moved him temporarily into my condo, and took him around Seattle and showed him how to use its public transportation system, and located a job for him in a deli. Together we found him a twelve-step program for drug addicts in recovery.

He lives nearby in an apartment I hunted down for him, and we have gone on with our lives. I call him almost every night, whether I am here or away on business. Slowly, he is taking charge of his life. It seems a shame to say so, but because the light in his soul is diminished, the one in mine, out of sympathy, is diminished too. I cry occasionally, but unsentimentally, and we still take pleasure in bickering, as we always have. His inflammations still cause him pain, and he moves now with small steps like an old man, but when I am in town I bring him dinners from Trader Joe's and magazines from the drugstore, and, one night, he brought over a sandwich for me that he himself had made at the deli. As I bit into the rye bread and corned beef, he watched me. "You like it?" he asked.

"It's fine," I said, shrugging. "Sauerkraut's a bit thick."

"That's how I do it," he said crossly, full of rehab righteousness.

"And I like more Russian dressing than this." I glanced out the window. "Moon's out," I said. "Full, I think. Werewolf weather."

He looked at it. "You never see the moon," he said, "until you sit all night watching it and you see how blindly stupid and oafish it is. I used to talk to it. My whole autobiography. Looked like the same moon I saw in Africa, but it wasn't. Never said a damn word in return once I was here. Over there, it wouldn't shut up."

"Well, it doesn't have anything to say to Americans," I remarked, my mouth full. "We're beyond that. Anything on TV?"

"Yeah," he said, "junkie TV, where people are about to die from their failings. Then they're rescued by Dr. Phil and put on the boat to that enchanted island they have." He waited. I got the feeling that he didn't believe in his own recovery. Or in the American project. Maybe we weren't really out of the woods.

"Okay, here's what I want you to do," he said. "I want you to call up Benny Takemitsu and tell him that I owe him some money." He laughed at the joke. Even his eyes lit up at the prankster aspect of making amends and its bourgeois comforts. "Tell him I'll pay him eventually. I'll pay him ten cents on the dollar."

"That's a good one."

"Hey, even Plato was disappointed by the material world. Me too."

"Gotcha."

"Pour me a drink," he commanded. I thought I knew what he was going to do, so I gave him what he wanted, some scotch with ice, despite my misgivings.

"Here's how you do it," he said, when he had the scotch in his hand. "Remember what they did in Ethiopia, that ceremonial thing?" He slowly upended the drink and emptied it out on my floor, where it puddled on the dining room tile. "In memory of those who are gone. In memory of those down below us."

It felt like a toast to our former selves. I looked out at the silent moon, imagining for a moment that he would be all right after all, and then I remembered to follow along. You're supposed to do it outside, on the ground, not in a building, but I inverted my beer bottle anyway. The beer gurgled out onto the floor, and I smiled as if something true and actual had happened, this import-ritual. Quinn smiled back, triumphant.

LIKE PENELOPE

by LUDMILLA PETRUSHEVSKAYA

There once lived a girl who was beloved by her mother but no one else. The girl was used to it and didn't get too upset. Her name was Oksana—a glamorous, fashionable name—but our heroine wished for something plainer: Tanya or Lena or even Xenia. She was a serious-minded young lady, tall but not very graceful.

Oksana studied forestry at a third-tier college—the only one she could attend for free. Upon graduating she could expect to get a clerical job in a state agency tallying birches and firs on paper. She and her mother shared a two-room apartment in a standard concrete building. In one respect their housing situation stood out: right below them, on the third floor, lived an incredibly noisy family of violent alcoholics. Every night the floor shook with screams, banging, and knocking; the lady of the house regularly interrupted her partying to stumble outside and yell "murder" and "help." Oksana tiptoed past their ravaged door; outside she dressed in dark clothing and wore her hat low over her face.

This was because she came home late, when it was already dark: she had the precious opportunity to take an affordable evening English class her school had introduced. Her mother told her about a certain Vladimir Lenin, who had learned a new language by translating a page of text into Russian and then back into the language, and Oksana adopted Lenin's method, translating the texts about logging, rafting, and skidding that the class provided—clearly, her college expected its students to haul timber on the Thames. The students protested, insisting that England didn't need Russian loggers with college degrees, and begged to be taught normal spoken English.

At that time, Oksana's mother was unemployed. She had set aside her hopes of being hired as an editor and was trying to pick up at least some copyediting. She called publishers and received "test assignments": a novel in two volumes, an action thriller of five hundred pages, a pharmacology textbook. Two weeks per project. At first Nina Sergeevna laughed at these assignments and their illiterate language and quoted the best lines to Oksana: "a passerby passed by" or "he was sitting on a seat." Driven by professional pride, she stayed up all night rewriting these miserable tomes down to the last comma. But when she tried to reach her so-called employers, she always ended up speaking to their secretaries, who told her that, alas, she hadn't passed the test. Oksana rightly suspected that these so-called publishers were taking advantage of her mother's free labor. To make ends meet, Nina Sergeevna worked as an attendant at a day care center, where she shared a tiny unheated booth with an overfed mongrel, a kind of guard dog who never left her quilted blanket and responded with nervous barking to the voice of the teacher behind the thin wall.

Soon this existence, already meager and not very happy, changed for the worse. One night there was a long-distance call: it was Klava, the mother of Nina Sergeevna's first husband, who had died very young, calling from Poltava in Ukraine. This Klava had continued to visit Nina even after she remarried and had Oksana; Klava used to bring them bags of boys' clothes that had belonged to her grandson Misha. Before long Misha's father, Klava's younger son, was lost to her too. Misha's mother remarried and moved to Israel, but Misha refused to leave his school and friends and moved in with Klava. For years Oksana had to wear Misha's hand-me-downs, including an emerald tuxedo with padded shoulders that made her cry. Oksana had never met Misha, but she couldn't stand him. And there you have the background to the midnight call.

The former mother-in-law informed Nina Sergeevna in an expressionless, metallic voice that Misha had lost everything; people whom he owed money had taken over his company. Klava had been forced to sell her apartment and move into a summer shack. The shack is made of plywood, Klava droned, the water and power are turned off after the summer, and someone has filled her well with trash. The firewood has run out; she had tried to burn tree branches, but they wouldn't burn. The cold has been incredible this winter—already it's started snowing. She

had gone to the city to collect her pension, but steered
clear of her former building: Misha had told her she might
be taken hostage if someone recognized her. A happy New
Year to you all, Klava concluded her monologue.

Nina Sergeevna used the pause to invite Klava to
come stay with them, then hung up the phone and stared
with her big eyes at her tall daughter, who stared back.
"Here we go again," concluded Oksana with a sigh. She
was used to her mother's almost daily acts of irrational
charity. The most recent one had occurred, in fact, just the
day before, at the Belorussky Station. Nina Sergeevna had
been crossing the bridge, sadly contemplating her editorial
career that had ended in a guard's booth, when in front of
her she noticed a tall woman with ramrod-straight posture
who walked woodenly and carried a pile of snow on her
head like a Pushkin monument. Nina Sergeevna bypassed
the strange creature and hurried toward the warm metro
station. But the woman caught up with her and asked if
she was going to Minsk—because she was; that is, she
wanted to, but she had no money—she'd been cheated.
She'd come from Belarus, she said, and brought with her
some cosmetics for sale, but the buyer hadn't shown up,
and she wasn't paid. The woman produced a Belarusian
passport. Nina Sergeevna told her to come inside the metro
station, it was too cold to talk in the street, but the woman
looked at her in terror: "Are you going to give me away
to the cops?" Ah, of course! The poor thing didn't have a
Moscow registration—she could be arrested at the entrance
to the subway. Nina Sergeevna asked how much she needed
to get home. The poor woman tried to calculate: five
hundred thousand, no, three hundred thousand, no, three
hundred rubles! Nina Sergeevna gave her the money and

also a baguette she'd been carrying home. Three hundred rubles was exactly one third of what remained of her pension after paying the rent. Thank god the monument hadn't asked for five hundred or a thousand—Nina S. would have satisfied any request for help. Often she didn't wait for people to ask and just gave away what she had.

Two days later they picked up Baba Klava at the station. Baba Klava had some luggage with her: the familiar backpack with summer work clothes from her dacha, two paper icons, and a sack of apples. Misha the grandson had forbid her to go back to the apartment, and as a result Klava had not a stitch of winter clothing and was wearing a summer shirt in December.

At Nina Sergeevna's, Klava installed her paper icons behind the glass front of the bookcase. She prayed to them constantly yet, she believed, discreetly. Her apples were left to rot under the kitchen table: Klava expected them to ripen by New Year's Eve. She shared Nina Sergeevna's sofa bed in the walk-through room but couldn't sleep— instead she did her best to lie still between Nina Sergeevna and the wall. Meanwhile the tired Nina and Oksana slept dreamlessly, treasuring every moment of rest.

Nina Sergeevna got back in touch with a half-forgotten friend who dabbled in philanthropy. That friend helped her get an appointment at a decent secondhand store, and Nina brought home a warm jacket and two quilted house robes for Klava, and also a length of light, gold-toned material—a former curtain. Oksana asked her mother sharply what the rag was for—they had plenty of rags as it was. "They offered; I took it," explained Nina S. innocently. "Looks like silk, almost."

Later Klava reluctantly recounted the tragic events

that had led to her homelessness. Misha the grandson had a small publishing business that printed calendars. He'd wanted to expand, and so he put out an expensive monograph by a Moscow artist (who had convinced Misha that he was the artist of the moment). The book didn't sell, and Misha owed money all around. The meter was ticking, and finally his creditor sent "shakers"—thugs who shake out money.

By then Oksana was taking classes part-time, in the evenings, and had found work at a landscape-design company. Graduation was postponed by two years. She was paid very little but did impeccable work for both the owner and the bookkeeper. What Oksana missed most was her English class. Every day she placed the same book in her purse, *The Hound of the Baskervilles*, and tried to read it on the train, but she always dozed off after a few lines.

In her free time Nina S. worked on getting poor Baba Klava recognized as a Russian citizen or at least a legal resident, so she could see a doctor. Moscow's plutocracy treated Klava as a foreign spy, simply because she was Ukrainian, and denied her all rights. After talking to fellow sufferers in endless lines, Nina decided she needed to go to Poltava to get a piece of paper from the local archive saying Klava had been born in Stavropol and was therefore a Russian citizen. Klava froze up. She was terrified the shakers would find out her address in Moscow. When the exhausted Nina returned with the necessary paper in hand, Klava asked in a fearful whisper whether Nina had visited her house. "Of course not!" Nina told her lightly. "I only stopped by the city hall and came right back. You will now receive your citizenship and a pension!"

When Klava went to watch television, Nina explained

to Oksana that she had visited Klava's courtyard and chatted with some neighbors, that was all. Told them she was a Muscovite wanting to move to Poltava—were there any apartments for sale in that building? Nothing, they told her. But, she said, apartment ten had just been sold, she'd heard. No comment. When she was leaving, one of the women caught up with her and took her phone number. Oksana almost fainted. "When will you learn to think? Why did you give that woman our number?"

"You know how I can read people!"

"That's right, you read that monument from Belarus the other day real well."

"This woman mentioned Klava: she remembered Misha, as well, and his father and mother, too. She used to work as a pediatric nurse—she treated Misha as a child! I knew what I was doing."

"Oh, Mama. I bet we'll have visitors soon." And Oksana was right.

Late at night on December 28, the phone rang out with long-distance calls. "Oksana, get Klava, quick!" Nina Sergeevna yelled, when she picked it up. Klava's body formed a little bump under a heavy blanket. The bump was trembling. "Who is it?" Oksana asked. "Shakers?" "No, no, it's Misha's mom calling from Jerusalem!"

As soon as Klava said "Hello" in her metallic voice, the connection broke. "Couldn't bear to speak to me," she said, putting the phone down. "Finally remembered her son. Too late—he's probably gone." And Klava marched off to the bathroom.

The next day Oksana brought home from her office a small potted juniper—a Christmas tree. "Oh, juniper," Klava whispered solemnly. "Just like the one on our family gravesite. My two sons are there, and my dear husband. Thank you, Oksanochka." Klava's mood was solemn these days. She loved watching TV police dramas in which justice temporarily triumphed. They calmed her down but didn't make her any more optimistic.

Nina Sergeevna was busily working on the piece of almost-silk from the secondhand store. The prerevolutionary Singer filled the little apartment with knocking. Klava went back to the kitchen, where she was making a holiday pie with the rescued dacha apples. Oksana was trying to study in her little room when Nina Sergeevna appeared with a pile of golden fabric.

"Our New Year's present to you, honey," she tentatively addressed her stern daughter. "To wear when you go out!"

"Mama! Stop imagining things! I'm not going out, and I'm not wearing this!"

"But, honey, Klava worked on it, too! She used to be a professional tailor. Remember the green tuxedo? She made it herself!"

"Tuxedo... Mama! I have finals in two weeks! My boss wouldn't give me any time off! She says she can't afford to give me time off—she's supporting a husband. She yelled at me for an hour. Now think, Mama: Do you really believe I can be interested in your refurbished garments?"

Klava walked into the room, saw the heap of silk, pursed her lips, and whispered, "Sorry, Oksanochka, I used to sew well, but my hands are not what they used to be. Nina, I told you she wouldn't wear it!" She turned back to the walk-through room and loudly began to pray.

Oksana glanced at the clock: an hour before New Year's. She took a bath, then sat down with wet hair at her old computer. Nina Sergeevna stroked her shoulder. "Please, baby. Klavochka is terribly upset that you won't even try it on. What will it cost you? She is eighty years old!"

From Klava's room came loud mumbling. Oksana gave in. In the bathroom, in front of the little mirror, she changed into the new dress. It was a very open evening gown with a slip and a weightless scarf to cover her bare shoulders. The scarf's edges had been embroidered by Nina Sergeevna. For goodness sake, thought Oksana, why did she waste her time on this embroidery? Who's going to see it? Who's going to see me? Her future of endless toil, without romance or glamour, flashed before her eyes. A messy office with bookkeeper Dina, an aging beauty from the provinces whose daughter refused to speak to her; her boss Olga, an emaciated workhorse with bags under her eyes, darting from client to client in a broken-down car. And the clients, wives of the new Russians, with their dreams of garden gnomes and potted junipers as seen in soap operas and their contempt for simple Russian trees. Suddenly Oksana reached for her never-used cosmetics purse and brushed her lashes thickly with mascara, shook out her damp hair to create a wave, applied her mother's blush to her cheekbones, and painted her lips generously. Why she was doing all this, for whom, Oksana didn't know. New Year's Eve. New dress. Black hair down to her waist. Big, rosy mouth.

Oksana stepped into the hall. The usual bangs and screams could be heard from the apartment downstairs. Oksana opened the door to her mother's room. Nina's eyes widened. "Klavochka!" she yelled in the direction of the kitchen. "Come here! Our princess has put on your dress." Klava pursed her lips into a tight smile and announced, "Like Penélope like Cruz!" The Moscow "like" had become Klava's default expression of strong emotion. Nina Sergeevna laughed with delight. "Once, at the dacha, years ago," she said, "we all decided to go mushroom-picking, and our neighbor Vera, she was at least eighty at the time, dashed over to the mirror and started painting her lips. My mother says to her, 'Aunt Vera, we are going to the woods; who's the lipstick for?' And Vera says—I'll never forget it—'Who knows? Maybe that's where IT will happen!'"

Klava pursed her lips again, Oksana shrugged, and the doorbell rang. Nina opened the door a crack and saw a strange young man.

"A happy New Year to you, Ma'am," said the man. "You should call the cops: somebody's getting killed downstairs."

"Don't worry, the cops stopped coming here a long time ago. They'll come when someone finally dies, they told us," said Oksana's mother, shutting the door and then rushing to the kitchen, where the chicken was burning. The doorbell rang again and kept on ringing. Oksana sighed, grabbed the phone, and shuffled to the door. Alcoholics are human, too, she thought—let them use the damn phone. The young man was still standing on the doorstep, holding his expensive leather suitcase. When he saw Oksana, his jaw dropped. "Excuse me," he mumbled, "may I speak with you?" "What is it?" Oksana asked impatiently. Suddenly Klava began screaming, "Misha!" Downstairs a man drunkenly yelled, "Friend, friend, come back!" and a woman begged them to call an ambulance— their own phone had been disconnected. Klava continued screaming, "Misha, is that you?" The stranger nodded silently, staring at Oksana, unable to say a word. "May I come in?" he finally asked—the voices from downstairs were approaching. Oksana sighed and stepped aside.

"Babushka, please stop yelling; let me get my coat off," said Misha. Then he addressed Oksana: "May I ask your name, Miss?" Oksana looked at him with her enormous eyes, straightened her long neck, and answered quietly, "Xenia."

"Xenia," repeated Misha. "What a lovely name. I need nothing else in this life."

Klava was brought to the scene. Ahs and ohs, hugs and kisses followed, along with Misha's assurances that Klava would have a new apartment, that everything would be taken care of—here are some presents for everyone.

Mama Nina observed her daughter and wondered where this new slow grace in her movements had come from, the twinkles in her laughing black eyes, the wave in her hair, the gorgeous dress... Of course: she had made it herself.

Translated by Anna Summers

BURNING BRIGHT

by T.C. BOYLE

TARA

She was born in captivity at an English zoo in 1978, one of a litter of three Bengal tiger cubs. Once she was weaned, she was tranquilized, lifted into a cage and flown across Europe, the Middle East and the Indian Ocean to Delhi, where she was put in the back of a pickup truck and driven north to the Dudhwa National Park in Uttar Pradesh, not far from the Nepalese border. There she came under the care of Billy Arjan Singh, hunter turned conservationist, who'd had success in rewilding leopards and now wanted to try his hand with tigers—not out of any sort of vanity, as with the maharajas and nouveaux riches who bred tigers for their own sport, but as a practical measure to reinvigorate the gene pool and save the species from extinction. The sad truth was that by then there were more tigers in captivity than in the wild.

He gave Tara the run of his house and yard, which was hemmed in by the serried vegetation of the park surrounding it, and he took her for excursions into the jungle in order to acclimate her. The first time the superintendent saw her ambling along at Billy's side, he called out, "Why, she's just like a dog." And Billy, grinning, ran a hand through the soft fur at her throat.

"She's just a big kitty," he called back. "Aren't you, darling?" And then he bent to her and let her lick the side of his face with the hot wet rasp of her tongue.

At first he fed her slabs of meat hacked from donated carcasses, then progressed to living game—rats, geese, francolin, civets—working up the food chain till she was stalking and running down the swamp deer and sambar that would constitute her natural prey. When she came into maturity—into heat—she left him to mate with one of the males he'd heard coughing and roaring in the night, but a few months later she allowed him to follow her to her den beneath the trunk of a downed sal tree and examine her first litter, four cubs, all apparently healthy.

What the tiger felt can only be imagined, but certainly to be removed from an enclosure in a cold alien place and released into the wild where her ancestors had roamed free through all the millennia before roads and zoos and even humans existed must have been gratifying in some deep atavistic way. Billy's feelings are easier to divine. He felt proud, felt vindicated, and for all the naysayers who claimed that captive-bred animals could never be reintegrated into the wild, here was Tara—and her cubs—to prove them wrong.

Unfortunately, two problems arose that Billy hadn't foreseen. The first was that the zoo in England had kept inaccurate stud records—shoddy, that is—so that genetic testing of her siblings would eventually show that Tara was not in fact a pure-bred Bengal but rather a hybrid whose father was of a different subspecies altogether—a Siberian. Billy's critics rose up in condemnation: he'd polluted the gene pool, whether intentionally or inadvertently, and there was no going back. The animals were at large and the damage was done.

Still, this was nothing compared with the second problem. Within six months of Tara's release, a resident of one of the local villages—a young woman, mother of four—was killed and partially eaten by a tiger that emerged in daylight and stalked down the center of the main street as if it had no fear of people whatever.

SIOBHAN

Her mother was going to keep a tight leash on her—that's what she'd said, what she'd been saying all week, as the house swelled with relatives and the presents mounted and the flowers filled every vase in the living room and the family room and spilled out onto the patio too. Siobhan was in the sixth grade and she didn't need any sort of leash, tight or loose, because she was dutiful and good and did what she was told, or mostly, anyway. It was her mother. Her mother was in a state, yelling into her cell phone at the caterers, the florist, even the Unitarian minister she'd picked out to perform the ceremony. If anybody needed a leash it was her.

Siobhan tried not to let it bother her. What she focused on, dwelled on, called up as if in some secret fantasy of glamour and excitement no one could begin to enter but her, was the fact that in less than an hour she would be leading the bridesmaids down the aisle at her sister's wedding, dressed in a mint-green taffeta gown she'd picked out herself. Plus, it was New Year's Eve; there would be fireworks at the pier and her mother had promised her she could stay up till midnight. Even better—and this had been the subject of a stream of breathless texts to her friends in Mrs. Lindelof's class for the past month—was where the wedding was being held. It wasn't going to be in a church or some cheesy reception hall or somebody's backyard, but in the outdoor pavilion at the San Francisco Zoo, where you'd be able to hear the animals cooing and trumpeting and roaring just as if you were in the jungle. It was the coolest thing she'd ever heard of.

She and her mother and father and Aunt Katie had the limo, a white one, longer than two cars put together, all to themselves. There was a bar in it, with Coke and 7Up and liquor and little packages of pretzel sticks, M&M's, and macadamia nuts. "Don't," her mother had warned as they pulled away from the house, snatching at her hand as she reached for the M&M's. "The last thing I need is to have you with chocolate smears all over your dress."

The last thing. Everything was the last thing, everything she did. But her mother was distracted, holding three conversations at once, with Aunt Katie and her father on either side of her and with Megan on the cell because Megan was in the other limo with her bridesmaids, and before they'd gone two blocks Siobhan had managed to stuff three crinkling packages of M&M's into her purse.

Very carefully, watching for her moment, she snuck a
handful of the candy-coated pellets into her mouth. Her
mother's eyes, framed in eyeliner like an actress's, were
huge, twice the size of normal, and they flared from one
thing to another, out the window, to the back of the
driver's head, to Aunt Katie, her father, but not to her, not
then, not while the chocolate lay secretly on her tongue,
the dark rich savor melting away because she didn't dare
chew, the excitement building in her like a beating drum.

"You damn well better," her mother said into the
phone, and then ended the call. "I don't know, Tom," she
went on, her voice jerking at the words as if each one was
attached to a string that went all the way down her throat.
"I don't know. I really don't."

Aunt Katie—young, blond, pretty, with a face just like
Siobhan's mother's, only without all the lines—said, "It's
all right. Everything's fine. Relax, Janie, just relax."

Her father let out a curse. "Christ," he said. "What is it
now, exactly?"

"I just can't get used to it."

"What? Oh, shit, don't tell me—"

"Dylan's father, with those teeth. And the mother—
she's the nicest person, it's not that, but she's so pushy
and now we have to sit around and eat, I don't know, sea
cucumber and squid at our own daughter's reception—"

"Just say it—they're Chinese, right? Well, I've got
news for you—they've been Chinese since the kids started
dating. Can't you give it a rest? Or are you going to go
ahead and spoil it for everybody?"

"I know, I know: you're right. But she's so dark. And
short. Even in heels. I mean, really, have you *looked* at her?"

"What are you talking about? Who?"

But her mother, her eyes bugging like those cue-ball eyes the boys always brought to class on the last day of school, just jerked her head to stare out the window, both her feet in their ivory patent-leather heels tapping so furiously it sounded as if the limo was falling apart.

VIJAY

A week earlier, on Christmas Day, he'd awakened feeling rinsed out and headachy, just maybe half a beat away from getting up and being sick in the toilet. He'd made the rounds of the parties the night before with his older brother Vikram, who was twenty-one and already had his associate's degree in pharmacology, and his best friend, Manny, who was his classmate at Lincoln High. There'd been pot and plenty of booze, tequila and vodka mostly. And beer, too, of course—beer was like water to him now. He could drink with the best of them—had been drinking since his sophomore year—and he didn't get silly or weepy like some of the retards in his class and he didn't let it affect his grades either. He'd applied to Berkeley, Davis, and San Diego State as his first-choice schools and six backup schools too, and he intended to get into at least one of the top three and win a scholarship while he was at it. But right now everything was a little hazy and the smell of his mother's cooking seeping in under the door didn't make things any better.

Curry. The eternal curry. But then why should she cook anything special today, which meant nothing to them, after all? If Jesus had gone and gotten born on some date approximating this one two thousand years ago and then went on to get nailed to the cross, sacrificed like a lamb or

some Hazuri goat, what did it matter? His parents were
Sikhs, both of them born in Punjab, and he and Vikram
were American, pure and simple. All the hocus-pocus
of priests and incense and kneeling and chanting that
Manny's family bought into as if it were the biggest thing
in the world was beyond irrelevant. He'd seen it, firsthand.
He'd gone to the big drafty church on Ashton Avenue for
Manny's confirmation when he was fourteen, and while
the whole thing was interesting in a kind of anthropolog-
ical way—Manny in a suit, Manny mumbling back at the
priest, Spanish and Latin and English all leaching into one
another, people dipping their fingers in a trough of water
that was no different from what came out of the tap except
that it had been blessed by the priest—it was the party
afterward that had lit him up. There was a piñata. Tamales.
And Manny's father—because this was an initiation and
they were grown up now—allowed them each a glass of
thin red wine that tasted like the wax of the white candles
blazing over the shrine in the living room.

The sheets felt stiff. And there was a smell, a vague
nameless funk that seemed to rise around him every time
he shifted position. Were they stained? Had he come home
and masturbated last night? He couldn't remember. He
lay there a moment longer, then pushed himself up and
went into the bathroom across the hall and drank down
two glasses of water. Vikram's door was closed. What time
was it? It felt late, past breakfast anyway. He padded back
into his bedroom and pulled his cell from the front pocket
of his jeans and checked the time: 12:30. Then he thought
of his mother downstairs cooking and his father, on this
universal day off, sitting there in front of the TV, watching
soccer on the Spanish-language channel, though he didn't

understand a word of it—*What do I care, Vijay? I see the ball, I see the referee, I see the ball go into the net*—and, on an impulse, he hit Manny's number.

"Hey," he said, when Manny answered.

"Hey."

"How you feeling?"

"I don't know. Hungover. How about you?"

He shrugged, no big deal, though Manny wasn't there to see it. "Maybe a little. But I gotta get out of here today, I think. You done with the family stuff?"

"I don't know, sure. What do you got in mind?"

"There's nobody going to be at the zoo today, it'll be like *deserted*, so I thought, once I tear Vik away from his sexy dreams, maybe we just go over there and hang out, you know?"

No response. But he could hear Manny breathing on the other side.

"We can like grab a burger on the way. And Vik still has that Stoli from last night—so even if the stores are closed... And weed—weed, of course. What do you say? You cool with it?"

TATIANA

She was a Siberian, four and a half years old, with the wide head, heavy frame, and pale fur that distinguished her subspecies of *Panthera tigris*. Like Tara, she'd been born in captivity—at the Denver Zoo—and then transferred to San Francisco for breeding purposes two years later. That first day, when she came out of sedation, she found herself in the same cage she'd been forced into just before dawn in the thin dry air of the Rocky Mountains, the only air she'd ever known, but there was something different about the cage now and it took her a moment to apprehend it: the front panel stood open. The smell must have come to her then, dank and lingering, the reek of the sea that was less than a quarter mile away, and then all the other smells she would have recognized from that morning and the morning before and all the mornings of her life, animal smells, the scent of urine and feces and the riveting anal discharge big cats use to mark their territory.

She didn't emerge right away, not that first day. She seemed to prefer the cage, with its impermeable top and the fading odors of her home, safe there from whatever loomed above the high concrete walls of the outdoor enclosure in which her cage had been placed. Sounds came to her: the harsh broken cries of parrots and macaws, the noise of traffic out on the street and of the engines of the planes that were like insects droning across the sky, the trumpeting of an elephant, a snarl, a roar, and over it all the screeching of monkeys, monkeys and apes.

VIJAY

He hadn't confessed it to anyone, not even his brother, because he wasn't a dork and didn't want to be taken for one, like all the other Indians and Chinese he'd been lumped together with in school since kindergarten, but his secret love, his true love, wasn't for the engineering degree his parents kept pushing him toward, but for animals. He wanted to be a zoologist—or better yet, a field biologist, studying animals in a state of nature, just like on the TV shows. Both Vik and Manny would say things like *Why the zoo all the time, man, what's the deal? You in love with a gorilla, or what?* And he would shrug and say *I don't know, you got a better suggestion?* And they didn't. Because the zoo was five blocks from the house, and he and Vik had been going there since they were kids, just to get out from under the critical eye of their mother, who would have objected if they were going to just hang out on the street like hooligans (*Hooligans and I don't know*, gangbangers, *isn't that what they call them?*), but found the idea of the zoo vaguely educational. To her it was a place where they weren't going to get in trouble.

By the time they got to the burger place on Sloat across from the zoo, it was already three in the afternoon and it just seemed natural to doctor their Cokes with a hit or two from the bottle, especially since it was a holiday and it was a hair-of-the-dog kind of thing, though Manny said it was disgusting to waste good vodka like that so he ordered an orange drink to go with his. It was a gray day, heavy with mist rolling in off the ocean. The burger place was deserted, the streets were empty. Christmas. They stared out the window on nothing, chewing.

"What time you got to be home?" he asked Manny. "It's like a special dinner today, right? With like your aunts and uncles and all that?"

Manny ducked his head, took a pull of his orange and vodka. He was in his board shorts and a black hoodie and he was wearing a brand-new Warriors cap, a Christmas present from his sister. "I don't know," he said. "Six, six-thirty. And yeah, I gotta be there."

Vik hadn't said much to this point, his eyes raw and red, his cheeks puffed out as if the burger was repeating on him. "Hey, if we're going to go," he said now, "we ought to go. Anybody comes by and sees us here they're going to think we're losers, right? Primo losers. And we can't smoke in here, anyway."

So they got up and shuffled out the door, Vijay secretly pleased it was his brother who'd got them motivated instead of him because he wouldn't want to seem too eager, but the fact was the zoo would be closing at dusk and they didn't really have all that much time. Out on the sidewalk, Vik lit a joint and they passed it hand to hand as they crossed the street to the zoo's entrance. "So Christmas," Vik was saying to Manny. "Do you have a tree and all that?"

Manny had his head down as if he had to watch his feet to be sure of where they were going. He seemed rocked already. "Yeah," he murmured.

"That cool?"

"Yeah. We put lights on it, ornaments. Colored balls."

"Spangles? Those silver things, I mean?"

"Tinsel, yeah."

They were almost at the ticket kiosk now, Vijay digging into his wallet for the family pass their mother renewed each year. All he had to do was flash it at whoever was behind the window, usually a bony red-haired girl with no tits and an onyx stud like a mole under her lip, and she just waved them in—Manny, with his dark skin and black buzz cut, passing for just another brother in the Singh family.

Vik said, "That's a German thing, you know."

"What, tinsel?"

"The tree. 'O Tannenbaum.' Didn't you guys have to sing that in elementary school?" Then he was laughing, one of those warm-up laughs that promised more but really wasn't out of control yet. "I mean, it's not Mexican or even American, but *German*. Can you picture it? All those Nazis handing out these scrawny little trees to cheer up the Jews at what, Auschwitz?"

They were there now, at the window, and Vijay was flashing the family membership card, and though the girl wasn't there—*Christmas*—but some fat old man instead, it wasn't a problem. He barely glanced up from his iPhone, the old man—fat, fat as a Butterball turkey stuffed with sausage and chestnuts and cranberries and whatever—fixing them for half a second with his beady brown dog's eyes, and then he waved them in.

SIOBHAN

Of course, the wedding didn't start right away (and the groom couldn't see the bride because that was bad luck), so she had to go into this little back room that looked like somebody's office with her sister and her friends, everybody putting on makeup and texting like mad and passing around a silver flask with sambuca in it. Nobody offered her any, and she wouldn't have taken it anyway, even out of curiosity, because liquor was for adults and she wasn't an adult and was in no particular hurry to be one. She did have a Red Bull, though, and it made her feel as if she were in the final lap of a race at school and beating everybody by a mile.

Then her mother came for them and they were outside in the damp air, the fog misting around them and the smell of the animals sharp in her nostrils. There was a hooting in the distance, one of the monkeys, the ones with voices like fire alarms. It just kept going, this monkey, and when you thought it was going to stop, when it slowed down and the hoots were softer and spaced further apart, it was only gathering breath for the next blast. That was the thing about having the wedding at the zoo—it was weird, but in a good way, because you never knew what was going to happen. Unlike in a church. Here was this thing out of a jungle someplace that didn't care in the slightest bit about them.

She was watching her feet now, as they came down the walk and under the roof of the open-air pavilion, afraid to trip or stumble or do something wrong, all the adults ahead of them standing up and looking back over their shoulders to get a glimpse of the bride, while the string quartet strained to drown out the monkey. All the men were in tuxedos. Some of the women wore hats. There were flowers everywhere. And then, just as she got to where the minister was waiting along with Dylan and the best man, she saw Dylan's little brother Jason, who was thirteen and a secret smoker of clove cigarettes, Jason, dressed in a suit and tie and giving her his starving zombie look to make her laugh. But she didn't laugh, though the Red Bull was pulsing through her. She just swept up the aisle the way she'd practiced it at the rehearsal, smiling at everybody as if she were the one getting married.

Afterward, when people were standing in line for food and drinks and the DJ was setting up his equipment, Jason came up to her with a plate of pot stickers and offered her one. "Did you hear that monkey?" he said. "I thought he was going to bust a gut."

She hadn't noticed till that moment that the sound was gone, long gone, replaced now by the prandial buzz of the adults poised over their plates and wineglasses. "It was *so* funny," she said, using her fingers to pluck a pot sticker from the edge of the plate.

"If any monkey knows any reason why these two should

not be joined together, let him speak now or forever hold his peace."

She laughed at the very moment she bit into the pot sticker, which caused a dribble of grease to run down the front of her dress. She glanced up guiltily to see if her mother was watching, but her mother was on the far side of the pavilion with Aunt Katie, waving a glass of yellowish wine as if it were a baton.

"Hey," Jason said, his smile narrowing till it was gone, "you want to see something?"

"What?"

He shot his eyes at the adults bent over their canapés and drinks, then came back to her. He lifted his chin to point behind her, down the steps of the pavilion toward where the walk wound its way into the depths of the zoo. "Out there, I mean?"

She didn't know what to say. The zoo was closed, yellow crime-scene tape—DO NOT CROSS—stretched across the path, and her mother had strictly forbidden her even to think for a single second about leaving the pavilion. Her mother meant it. The whole last week she'd been in a fury, constantly on the phone with her lawyer and the zoo people and the mayor's office and anybody else she could harangue. They'd threatened to cancel the permit for the wedding. Because of what had happened on Christmas. The accident. The attack. It was on the news, on Facebook, Twitter, everywhere—the police were investigating and the zoo was closed until further notice. But her mother had prevailed. Her mother had connections. Her mother always got what she wanted—and they'd reserved the pavilion a whole year in advance, because Megan and Dylan had met here at the zoo as interns on summer vacation from college

and it was the only place in the world they would even con-
sider exchanging vows. They'd hired the caterers, the DJ,
sent out invitations. There was only one answer her mother
would accept. Megan and Dylan got their pavilion, but the
rest of the zoo was off-limits. To everybody. Period.

She just looked at him. He knew the situation as well
as she did.

"I found something," he said. "On the walk there? It's
like two hundred feet away."

"What?" she said.

"Blood."

TARA

Typically, there had been one or two tiger attacks in the
reserve each year, usually during the monsoon season,
when people went into the park to collect grasses for their
animals. Over the years, going all the way back to the last
century, long before the park existed—and long before that,
too, as long as people and wild animals had been thrust
together in the same dwindling patchwork of bush and
farmer's fields—the region had had its share of man-eaters,
but these had been hunted down and eliminated.

Now, after the latest victims, two more from the nearest village, were found lying in a tangle of disarticulated
limbs along a path just a mile from the site of the first
attack, Billy Arjan Singh began to have second thoughts.
Publicly, he maintained that the attacks could have come
from any of the park's tigers, especially those that had been
injured or were too old and feeble to hunt their customary
prey—and Tara, demonstrably, was as young and vig-
orous as any animal out there—but privately he began

to admit the possibility that his experiment had gone terribly wrong.

There came a respite. Several months went by without report of any new victims, though one man—a wood-cutter—went missing and was never heard from again. Billy dismissed the rumor. People went missing all the time—they ran off, changed their names, hitchhiked to Delhi, flew to America, died of a pain up under the ribcage and lay face-down in some secret place till the jackals, carrion birds, and worms had done with them. All was quiet. He began the process of obtaining permits to bring another animal into the country, this one from the zoo at Frankfurt.

Then it all went to hell. A woman—a grandmother barely five feet tall—was snatched while hanging laundry out to dry and half the village witnessed it—and before the week was out, a bicyclist was taken. In rapid succession, all along the perimeter of the park, six more people were killed, always in daylight and always by a tiger that seemed to come out of nowhere. Outrage mounted. The newspapers were savage. Finally, Billy gave in to the pressure and mounted a hunt to put an end to the killings—and, he hoped, prove that it was some other animal and not Tara that was responsible.

In all, before the tiger—*a* tiger—was shot, twenty-four people lost their lives. Billy was there for the kill, along with two of the park's rangers, though when the tiger came to the bait—a goat bleating out its discomfort where it had wound itself around the stake to which it was tethered— his hand fluttered on the trigger. They followed the blood spoor to a copse and stood at a safe distance as the tiger's anguished breathing subsided, and then Billy moved in alone to deliver the coup de grâce. The animal proved to be young—and female—but it had no distinguishing marks; to the last, Billy insisted it wasn't Tara. Whether it was or not, no one will ever know, because he chose to bury the carcass there deep in the jungle, where the mad growth of vegetation would obliterate the evidence in a week's time. In any case, the attacks ceased and life in the villages went back to normal.

VIJAY

He always had specific things he wanted to see—the African savanna, where zebra, kudu, ostrich and giraffe wandered back and forth as if there were no walls or fences and you could watch them grazing, watch them pissing and shitting and sometimes frisking around; and the koalas, he loved the koalas, and the bears and the chimps, the little things that were different about them each time he visited—but Vik and Manny didn't care about any of that. For them the zoo was just a place where they could watch girls, get stoned, and kick back without anybody coming down on them. He didn't mind. He felt that way himself sometimes—today, for instance. Today especially. It was Christmas. They were out of school. He'd worked hard all term and now it was time to let loose.

They barely glanced at the savanna but went on into the primate center as if they'd agreed on it beforehand. There was hardly anybody around. The chimps looked raggedy, the gorillas were asleep. Vik wrinkled up his nose. "Man, it *stinks* in here. Don't these things ever take a bath?"

"Or use underarm deodorant," Manny put in. "They could at least use deodorant, couldn't they? I mean, for our sake?" And then he was lifting his voice till he was shouting: "Hey, all you monkeys—yeah, I'm talking to you! You got no consideration, you know that?"

And this was funny, flat-out hilarious, because they were all feeling the effects of the weed and weed made everything hilarious. He laughed till he couldn't breathe, Vik's face red and Manny's too.

"Remember the time," he was saying, trying to catch his breath, "like maybe two years ago or something, when we were here and those dudes were painting the cage?"

"Oh, yeah, yeah," Manny gasped, and they were all laughing again at the thought of it, the day they'd come into the ape house and there were two workers inside one of the empty cages, painting the back wall, and they'd all crowded up to the bars making jokes about the new species of ape on exhibit and how clever it was—*Look, it's Bigfoot, and look, look, it can dip a paintbrush, cooooool*—until one of the workers turned around and told them to go fuck themselves.

Was it really all that funny? Yes. Yes it was. Because it was a routine now and they could call it up anytime they wanted, the three of them united and the rest of the world excluded.

So they laughed, drifting from one exhibit to another, not really paying attention, and if there were any girls to look at they were few and far between. Because it was a holiday. Because it was Christmas. At some point they were out front of the snack bar—the *Leaping Lemur Café*, another joke—and Manny said he wanted a fresh orange drink to make the vodka go down and maybe some nachos. "Anybody want nachos?"

Vijay got himself a Coke because his throat was dry and watched the kid behind the counter pour a glob of neon-orange cheese over Manny's chips. The only other people there—a mother with a baby in a stroller and an older couple gobbling hot dogs—looked on as if the whole world had come to a stop. The kid behind the counter had the name of some pathetic metal band tattooed across the knuckles of his left hand—*Slayer*—but since there were six letters and only four fingers to line up, the *yer* had been squeezed in on the last knuckle, which was the smallest one, and what did that say about planning and foresight? Not to mention basic IQ?

After that, they drifted over to the big cats, hoping to see them up and about, if only for the sake of breaking the tedium, but the lions—a male and two females—were lying there unconscious. "Shit, look at them," Vik said. "They might as well be rugs."

"Zoned out," Manny said. And then he got up on the metal rail where you're not supposed to be and started waving his arms and shouting—"Hey, lions, hey! Hey, I'm *talkin'* to you!"

Vik joined in and this was funny too, the two of them goofing, the lions stretched out as if they were dead, the sky closing in and everything as dim and gray and depressing as only a winter's afternoon in San Francisco could be. They began to roar then, roar like lions, and he joined in just for the sheer crazy throat-rattling rush of it, but still the lions never moved, not even to twitch their tails. They all three roared till they were almost out of breath and then they broke down and laughed till they were.

Finally Vik straightened up and said, "I don't know— this is boring. I'm ready to bag it, how about you?"

Manny shrugged.

And then, surprising himself because it really didn't

matter one way or the other and they were going to have to
go home eventually, everybody knew that, he said, "What
about the tiger?"

SIOBHAN

Her mother wasn't watching, her mother was busy air-
kissing everybody and waving her wineglass, and once the
music got going people started dancing, which provided a
natural screen. She ducked away under the cover of swaying
gowns and tuxedoed shoulders and met Jason in the bushes
just off the path, where nobody could see them. "Come on,"
he whispered, taking her by the hand. "It's this way."

She could feel her heart going. Her mother would kill
her if she found out. Absolutely kill her. Plus this was
Jason, a boy two years older, and he was holding her hand.
He led her through a fringe of low palms and then back
onto the walk where it looped away out of sight of the
pavilion. It was dusk now and the bushes seemed denser,
dangerous suddenly, as if anything could have gotten loose
and hidden itself there in the shadows, waiting to spring
out at them. The birds were chattering, the ones in the trees
and the ones in the cages somewhere up ahead. Suddenly
Jason let go of her hand and darted up the path, his dress
shoes slapping at the pavement. She hurried on, nearly
frantic with excitement, the smells coming to her now, the
sounds of furtive movement, the low coughs and snorts
and muffled roars. But there he was, just ahead, down on
his knees and gesturing to her, the soles of his shoes palely
glowing and his suit jacket bunched at the shoulders. "Over
here," he said, trying to keep his voice down. "Hurry!"

When she came up to him she saw that he was bent

over a dark uneven stain on the concrete, a spot no bigger around than one of the desktops in school. "See it?" he whispered.

She looked down, leaned closer, then straightened up, hands on hips. "That's just a wet spot."

"Yeah?" he said. "And why do you think it's wet? And it's not just water, believe me"—and here he pressed his palm to the stain and then spread open his hand for her. "See that? See it? That's blood."

She saw nothing. Just his five fingers, the ones he'd wrapped around hers a minute ago, and his palm, which might have been slightly darker—or damper. "That's not blood," she said.

"Is so." He gave her a strained look, his features melting into shadow. The sound of the music from the pavilion suddenly came clear, drowning out the birds and whatever else was out there. He held her eyes and wiped his hands on his pants. "Diluted blood, anyway."

VIJAY

If the lions were comatose at this point, the tiger gave them what they wanted. The minute they appeared there at the edge of its enclosure—an open pit with a dry moat at the bottom of the wall and some fake rocks and a raked-over tree stump in the background—it looked up at them and started pacing. Or more than pacing—it was slinking, flowing like water from one place to another, its feet almost a blur and the muscles flexing hard in its shoulders. They all just stood there for a moment, watching it. He could feel the weed blurring things and the vodka trying to counteract it, burning through him. He felt rocked, dizzy almost, as if everything were floating a couple of inches off the ground. Vik said, "Now that's what they're supposed to do—give us some action. I mean we're paying customers, right? Or at least moms is."

And then, without warning, Vik jumped atop the restraining bar and began roaring down at the tiger. The effect was immediate: the tiger froze, staring up at him in confusion. Vik roared, flapped his arms. The tiger seemed to cringe, then its hackles rose and all of a sudden it was flowing faster, around and around, down into the moat below them and then back up and around again. Next thing Manny climbed up and they were both roaring and Manny started sailing nachos out into the void, one after the other, the tiger shrinking away from them as if they were on fire. "Kaboom!" Manny shouted. "Kaboom!"

They laughed. They were excited. And though Vijay knew it was wrong, knew they could get in trouble, knew the animals shouldn't be disturbed, let alone harassed, and that every sign warned against it, he found himself scrabbling around for something to throw—a pinecone, here was a pinecone in the dirt and he was snatching it up and rushing back to take aim. Why? He couldn't have said, then or afterward. It was something primal, that was all. They had this thing on the run, this big jungle cat that was as scared as the fluffed-up little Pomeranian in the apartment next door, and when the first pinecone went skittering across the concrete floor of the enclosure he took off running for another one, for a stick, for anything.

That was when he heard the sound Manny made. It wasn't a scream but something hoarser, deeper, worse—and he turned round to see the tiger's head burst up right there at the lip of the enclosure and the tiger's claws digging in, the big paws and clenched forearms clinging impossibly to the molded concrete for the smallest fraction of an instant before the striped flanks came surging into the picture and it was there like some CGI demon, grabbing hold of Manny and taking him down on the pavement in a quick thrash of limbs and a noise that was like a generator cranking up again and again. Vik's face. Manny down. The noise. And then the cat was on Vik and Vik was screaming and before he could think the thing was on him, tearing at the back of his neck and dropping him to the pavement as if he'd been sledgehammered. He was trying to ball up and protect his head, the smell of blood and rot and the froth of saliva hot in his face, thinking nothing, thinking death, his shoulders and forearms raked and bitten and his feet a thousand miles away, when the tiger suddenly let go of him.

TATIANA

In the wild, a Siberian of Tatiana's age might have a range as extensive as sixty square miles, but she'd never been in the wild, had never known any place but this and the zoo in Denver, and her territory was measured in square feet, not miles. Industry standards vary on the minimum size of big-cat exhibits, but restraining walls are mandated at sixteen and a half feet, a height no tiger, no matter the provocation or duress, could ever hope to surmount. Unfortunately, in the aftermath of the incident at the San Francisco Zoo, the wall was found to be substandard, measuring just twelve and a half feet from the floor of the moat to its highest point.

SIOBHAN

She managed to make it back without her mother catching her—and what her mother didn't know would never hurt her, would it? That's what Jason said, anyway, and, giggling, she agreed with him as he led her to the bar through the dense swaying forest of adults, who were dancing now, their arms in motion and heads bobbing to the beat. The DJ was playing Beyoncé, Fergie, Adele, Megan's favorites. Megan was dancing with Dylan and the bridesmaids all had their boyfriends out on the dance floor now too. The bass was so strong it was like an earthquake and she could feel it thrumming through the soles of her shoes. People made way for them at the bar as if they were celebrities— and they were, or she was anyway, *flower girl*, sister of the bride—and she asked for a Diet Coke, no ice, and Jason got a club soda and cranberry with two cherries and a shot of grenadine, then they lined up at the food table for dim sum and ribs and still her mother never came looking for her.

Jason piled up his plate and then set it back down again on the table. "Oh, shit," he said, "I better go wash my hands. Watch my plate?"

"*Jason*, it wasn't blood."

He gave her a look of disbelief. He was tall for his age and his head seemed to bob up over his neck like E.T.'s, and she wondered about that, if she could give him a secret moniker—just two initials—when she texted Tiffany and Margaret to tell them she was hanging out with a boy at the wedding. She liked the way his hair was clipped in two perfect arches around his ears. She liked the way he was grinning at her now. "I wouldn't want to catch AIDS," he said, holding out his palms as if to deny it.

And then he was gone and she started eating by herself

at a table in the far corner of the pavilion, but when he came back, conspicuously wiping his hands on the legs of his suit pants, he picked up his plate and came right to her. They didn't say anything for a long while, eating in silence and staring out at the adults as if they were going to have to take a quiz on the party. She heard her mother's high whinnying laugh and the next minute her father was leading her mother out onto the dance floor and she watched them settle into some weird gyrating sort of dance they must have learned in college back in the seventies. "You know what?" she said. "I don't think I've ever seen my parents dance before."

"My parents would never dance," Jason said. She followed his eyes to where they sat stiffly in two chairs pushed up against the rail, Jason's grandmother just to the right of them and just as stiff. "Even if somebody picked up an AK and said 'Dance or die!'"

"What about you?" she asked and she felt her cheeks color. "I mean, do you dance?"

"Me?" He held the moment, straight-faced, before he broke into a grin. "I'm the number-one best dancer in the world," he said, letting his eyes flick over the dance floor before turning back to her. "Now that Michael Jackson's dead."

VIJAY

What he did, and it was nothing anybody in any movie he'd ever seen would have done, was run. As soon as the tiger let go of him—to slam back into Manny so hard it was like a rocket flashing across the pavement—he scrambled to his feet and ran as hard as he could through the gloom of the day that was closing down around him, looking frantically for a way out, a tree to climb, anything, before he realized he was making for the snack bar, where there were people, where they could call 911, call the cops, call an ambulance. He didn't think of Vik till Vik came pounding up behind him, blood all over, his clothes in strips and his eyes rolled back in his head. They didn't say anything, not a word, just ran. It was maybe three hundred yards to the snack bar, three football fields, but it seemed to take forever to get there, as if they were running in place in some waking nightmare—and that was what this was, exactly what it was.

But when they got there, frantic, the doors were locked and they could see the guy inside, the metalhead, the moron, and he wasn't moving toward them—*he was backing away!* Vik was beating on the glass, they both were, shouting for help, shouting to open up because there was an animal loose, a tiger loose, open up, open up!

The kid didn't open up. He just backed into a corner and tried to stare them down, but he had his cell in his hand and he was punching in a number (as it later turned out he *was* dialing 911, not because he believed them but because he thought they were on drugs and trying to rob the place). They kept beating on the glass and they would have broken right through it if they could, beating with the palms of their hands and shouting out for help, until they watched the kid's face go slack and turned to see the tiger coming right at them, its feet churning and its head down—following the blood trail, following the spoor. Vijay felt it like a hot wind as it blew past him to career into Vik, its paws raking and batting, and though he flattened himself against the glass, shouting "Vik! Vik!" there was nothing he could do but wait to die as the flashing teeth and furious claws worked his brother over.

TATIANA

This world. This world of apes, this screeching world. She
was out in it, terrified, enraged, doing the only thing she
knew to do, one down and dead and another beneath her,
all the power of all the generations invested in her and
burning bright. She roared. She showed her fangs. And she
would have gone for the other one, the one frozen there by
the shimmering wall, if it weren't for the distraction of this
solid rolling thing with its flashing lights and screaming
siren and the hot quick shock of surprise that ended
her life.

SIOBHAN

She danced till she was soaked through—and he was right,
Jason, he was the best dancer in the world. The music
seeped through her skin and into her blood. Her father
danced with her, then she danced with her sister and
everybody was taking pictures with their cell phones. And
then there was a slow song and Jason put an arm around
her waist and she watched what everybody else was doing,
all the adults, and rested her head on his shoulder, on his
chest, right where she could feel the flutter of his heart. She
couldn't hear any of the animals anymore, couldn't have
heard them even if they'd been roaring, because the music
was everything. The night settled in. Jason rocked with
her. And if she knew where she was at all, it was because
of the smell: the furtive lingering odor of all those animals
locked in their cages.

The United States penitentiary in Marion, Illinois, photographed by the author.

THE TEXAN FROM GAZA DOES YOGA IN PRISON

GHASSAN ELASHI RECEIVED A SIXTY-FIVE YEAR
SENTENCE AS PART OF THE MOST EXTENSIVE
TERROR-FUNDING CASE IN U.S. HISTORY.
HIS DAUGHTER SPENDS TWO DAYS WITH HIM
IN "GUANTÁNAMO NORTH"—THE FEDERAL
GOVERNMENT'S COMMUNICATION MANAGEMENT
UNIT, IN MARION, ILLINOIS.

nonfiction by NOOR ELASHI

DAY ONE

Baba learned yoga and Pilates in prison. He read somewhere that the postures were guaranteed to relieve tension, improve stamina, and increase endurance. Baba had, on many occasions, discussed his new practice, and now it was time to show us how hard he'd been working. It's a November day, and Baba has slipped off his shoes in preparation.

Like any father, he spotted the worry in his daughter's eyes, and sought to ease it. In response, I glanced away: at the eight-digit number stitched to his chest pocket, at the camera screwed into the top edge of the wall, at the

Plexiglas barrier that split the room in two. But when
I focused on Baba, none of it seemed to matter. It was
Thanksgiving, 2010, and this fifty-six-year-old Gaza City
native was getting ready for a mat workout, even though
he had no mat.

He began with the standing forward bend, which he
performed by stretching his arms up and forward, then
slowly descending until his palms were gripping the backs
of his ankles. "Try your best not to bend your knees," he
instructed, his voice muffled by the Plexiglas. He held the
position for several seconds, transitioning into a human
paperclip.

My two teenage brothers, despite their embarrassment,
were impressed. Mother kept praising the Lord, and Teta—
with apparent excitement—was repeating in her casual
Arabic, "Be careful, my son." I was twenty-four years
old and aware of the absurdity unfolding before me, but
I wanted to see more. Baba said he was only beginning.

With his legs directly in front of him, he repositioned
himself for the seated forward bend. "Remember to
breathe," he said, freeing his upper body until his forehead
rested on his shins. He grasped his feet, a move that
seemed unbearable, but his agile body bent with ease.

He went on to the plank, the cobra, and the half
tortoise pose. By this point, the pace of his breathing
had escalated, and the droplets of sweat on his face had
multiplied. But he was not finished. Should Baba be a
Broadway star, this would be his eleven o'clock number:
the *shirshasana*. A headstand.

His legs started off steady, pointing toward the ceiling,
but soon he was deliberately bending each knee like an
upside-down cyclist. My brothers laughed. Within his glass

box, as if he were a figurine of sorts, Baba landed on his feet in one smooth motion, explaining that the weight should fall on your arms and shoulders, not on your head. He stood near the Plexiglas and flashed his open hand.

"Five minutes," he said. "I can usually stay in that position for five minutes."

His hand was still in the air when the prison guards swarmed in.

"Mr. Elashi, what are you doing? We saw you making hand signals. And why is your phone on the hook?"

"I'm teaching them," explained Baba. His voice faltered. "I'm just teaching them yoga."

"Well, we need to be able to hear everything you're saying. So, pick up the phone."

Baba agreed to finish up his exercises with the phone off the hook.

My father, Ghassan Elashi, was part of what's been deemed the most extensive "terror-funding" case in U.S. history. He co-founded the Holy Land Foundation, a humanitarian organization, in the late 1980s; remaining involved as an unpaid board member, my father watched his project become the largest American Muslim charity. But in December of 2001, President Bush shut down the HLF by executive order. Then, in 2004, my father and four other men—dubbed the Holy Land Five—were charged with conspiring to provide "material support" to charities linked to designated terrorist groups.

This support came in the form of humanitarian aid to Palestinian charities that prosecutors claimed "worked on behalf of" Hamas. What was perplexing for the first jury—which returned no guilty verdicts and deadlocked on most counts—was that these Palestinian charities, called "zakat committees," also received funds from our own government agencies, most notably USAID (the U.S. Agency for International Development). And none of these committees, as my father's attorney John Cline argued, were in fact listed as designated terrorist groups by the Department of the Treasury. One juror went as far as questioning the credibility of the prosecution's key witness, an Israeli intelligence officer who testified as an expert under a pseudonym. Even so, a second trial, in 2008, ended with guilty verdicts. Baba received a sentence of sixty-five years. The case would go on to be unsuccessfully appealed at every level, until the Supreme Court, ending the possibility of any reversal, declined to hear it in October 2012.

Watching Baba practice his exercises, I almost forgot that this was not a studio, not a place to polish one's yoga and Pilates skills. This was a prison visitation room, about five feet wide by seven feet long. We were inside a Communication Management Unit, in what National Public Radio has called "Guantánamo North," since more than two-thirds of the inmate population was Middle Eastern and/or Muslim.

The Center for Constitutional Rights, based in New York City, had filed a lawsuit against isolation units like this one. When my father was transferred here seven months earlier, I discovered that the CMUs were created during the Bush administration, and that two now exist: this one, in Marion, Illinois, and another in Terre Haute, Indiana. They are both segregated units designed to closely monitor inmates and restrict them from communicating with the outside world, which includes their attorneys, their families, and the media. Baba has less than half the phone time he had before his transfer; now he is limited to two calls a week, fifteen minutes each, scheduled in advance and live-monitored from Washington, D.C. And he's allowed a quarter of the visitation time that he was offered previously: two non-contact visitations a month.

DAY TWO

The fifteen-minute ride from the hotel to the prison had the kind of view remarkable for its downstate Illinois averageness, an ongoing canvas of flat, dry land spotted with clusters of cattle and capped with a dull autumn sky. The homes, although visibly occupied, were far apart and seemed to possess a bleak loneliness, amplified by the rain. After driving by the CMU's deserted checkpoint, our car approached a stop sign—but this wasn't your typical stop sign. This was where Justice Drive met Prison Road.

"I'm getting out," I said.

"Why?" Mother asked.

"Because I need to document this."

"They can probably see you."

"No, they can't."

"Trust me, Noor."

"Don't worry. It's just a picture."

Zipping up my jacket and setting my iPhone on camera mode, I stepped out of the car. I captured a few close-ups of the signs, and a few shots of my fourteen-year-old brother Sami leaning against the pole. He took some of me making a confounded face while pointing at the street names. Then we raced back to the rental car, feeling uplifted despite being soaking wet.

The architecture of the prison facade, with its gray diamond pattern, resembled that of a small abandoned museum. The visitation was scheduled for 10 a.m., which meant we had precisely seventeen minutes to park the car, sign in, clear the metal detectors, sprint down the hallway painted with its misplaced bright green stripe, pass through the common visitation area, and finally enter the room with the Plexiglas barrier. I greeted the man behind the front desk, the same pleasant man with the prominent eyebrows who had been stationed there the day before, and quickly started to fill out the requisite paperwork. When I looked up, I saw new uniformed figures—a fat smirking fellow and a slim female guard.

"Ma'am, we were informed that you were taking pictures of our facility," said the smirking fellow, whose strict tone came across as jolly when coupled with his Southern accent.

I thought for a moment, but before I could utter a word, Mother interjected.

"She's writing a book. She was just doing research for her book."

I stared at Mother with a face that begged to ask, Why would you say that? But seeing that the two guards were waiting for my answer, I turned to them and said, "I didn't take photos of your facility. I just took pictures of some street signs."

"Ma'am, for security reasons, we're going to have to see those photos," he said.

"Can we do this afterward? I'd rather not take time away from my father's visitation," I said.

"It'll only take a minute, Ma'am," he said.

"All right," I said. "I'll be right back."

The slim female guard stepped forward. "Actually, we're coming with you."

"You want to follow me to the car?" I asked.

"Yes," they both replied.

My fifteen-year-old brother, Mohammad, insisted on coming, too. This was more unexpected than being followed by the security duo. I'd been away from my brothers for almost a year and a half, in New York to pursue an MFA, but I clearly remembered their confusion, in my father's absence, their outbursts and their threats to run away. It was striking to see the young men they had become. Somehow, walking alongside my brother, a blue-eyed, straight-jeans-clad former skateboarder and soccer champion, made me feel less demoralized. What are siblings but an intolerable yet indispensable part of your flesh?

When we returned to the car, I flipped through the photos one by one, while the man with the smirk decided whether or not I could keep them. At one point a break in the clouds produced a subtle glare on the screen; he pulled it away from my hand, saying, "I can't really see what's on this machine right now." I discarded each of the street-sign photos, becoming gradually more disheartened as I went. The only pictures they let me keep were the ones of cows I'd taken the day before. On our way back to the prison lobby, the Southern guard told me that if the man in the tower caught me taking any more photos of their facility, I would be banned from visiting my father for an unspecified amount of time.

It was already after 10 a.m. We had smoothly passed through security the day before, but on this day each of us caused the metal detector to go off. The hallway's most prominent feature suddenly became the heap of barbed wire stretched out against the windows. And while yesterday Baba had been prepared and waiting on us when we entered the visitation room, today we had to wait twenty minutes for him to arrive.

By the look on Baba's face, I knew that there was some sort of new sadness brewing within him, but it wouldn't be until later that I would find out he was upset about the guards who had attempted to strip-search him after the previous day's visitation. Ever since Baba entered the prison system in 2007, he has explained to the various officers and wardens that according to his belief system, exposing private areas of his body was unconscionable; some of them have respected his plea, while others have chosen to ignore it. But the previous day's search had bothered Baba more than usual, because of its sheer pointlessness. Why subject him to it if he had no physical access to his family?

Even as he coped with this, Baba looked healthier than I'd seen him in years. His complexion had returned to its distinctive pale pink color, and he was back to a healthy weight. His hair and beard were now nearly white, and cropped short. The day before, he'd rolled up the sleeves of his khaki uniform to show Teta his toned biceps after she'd said, "Stay strong, my son." He'd also told my brothers, "Look, can you believe I have abs?" But he had declined to pull up his shirt to prove it.

Now he picked up the phone and started to greet us individually. Our side of the Plexiglas barrier provided just enough space to fit five chairs, organized in two rows. Leaving the room required that we stack the two chairs in back atop each other; otherwise, there was not enough room to open the door. As three of us spoke all at once, explaining to him why we had arrived half an hour late,

Baba realized that the receiver he held to his ear was not working. He shook the phone and gave it a few taps. But he heard only our muffled voices behind the glass. He put down the receiver. Before he could utter a word, a prison guard appeared at our door.

"Mr. Elashi, why aren't you using the phone? Pick it up now!"

"It's not working," Baba responded.

"What do you mean it's not working?"

"I mean, I can't hear my family."

"Let me in," the officer said. "I need to check on your phones."

So, to let him in, Teta and Mother had to squeeze into a corner while my brothers and I started to stack not just the two chairs in the back row, but the three others, as well. This was the only way to give the officer a clear path to the phones.

Somehow, after some tinkering, the phones were fixed. As the officer vacated our room, a guard with a goatee leaned toward Baba on the other side and slowly said, "Don't hang up the phone again."

Baba snapped. His face became dark red. "The phone wasn't working!" he shouted, standing up to close the door behind the guard. As we watched, the man held the knob and said, "Watch your tone, Mr. Elashi, or I will terminate your visit immediately."

"But the phone wasn't working!" Baba repeated, exasperated. When the door closed he waved his arm dismissively, as he usually does when he has nothing left to say.

Baba sat back down and forced a weak smile. Mother frowned and said, "Please, Ghassan, relax. I don't like to see you like this." I wanted to wrap my arms around him.

But I could only look at him and return his smile. When your conversations are measured in hours, it's imperative to not focus on what is negative, because it will consume you and further limit your already constricted time. So, the dialogue had no choice but go on, Teta relaying to Baba that so-and-so relative and such-and-such friend send their love, and Mother praising my three siblings who couldn't make the trip—my sister Huda, twenty, who'd just moved to Portland, Maine, to earn a doctorate degree in pharmacy; my sister Asma, nineteen and already applying to graduate school in speech pathology; and finally Omar, Mother's ten-year-old "right-hand man" with Down syndrome.

"I want them to be the best," Mother said, moving on to my brothers sitting beside her. "I want them to make us proud, but this one doesn't listen to me when I tell him, 'No more video games.' And that one refuses to study. He spends all his after-school time outside with the sheep."

Unlike us girls, who were born in California, the boys are thoroughly Texan. Mohammad owns a German shepherd, and Sami owns a lamb, and in the past, both of them had hinted at wanting to own farms. But in recent months, Sami had developed an obsession with the idea, which wouldn't have been so awful had he not also abandoned his schoolwork. Sami had concluded that being a farmer would not require a college degree.

Baba, looking closely at his second-eldest son, said, "I've written to you about this. Why don't you write me back?"

Sami, with his deep, strident voice, responded, "Because I feel ashamed."

I was surprised to hear him say it out loud. Nonetheless, he went on to admit that, yes, his grades could be better; but really he wanted only to buy around ten acres of land, grow some organic vegetables, raise cows and horses, maybe a few chickens, and just live off the earth.

"Does this make me weird?" he asked.

After thinking for a moment, Baba said, "Did you know that when I was your age, I had an organic garden?"

"Really?" said Sami, his eyes widening.

"Of course," said Baba. He had a faraway look in his eyes.

In the 1960s, Baba explained, he had lived in his grandparents' home, at the edge of a ten-acre orange grove in Adaraj, a suburb of Gaza City. His grandfather, whom he called Sido, grew oranges, tangerines, grapefruits, lemons, limes, apricots, plums, and even some palm trees. Sido had a garden bursting with color: yellow and red roses, jasmine, gardenia, olive trees, and grapevines. But most notably for Baba, the garden had a small lot he could call his own. In this square patch of land, Baba planted and tended cherry tomatoes, scallions, radishes, parsley, and fiery green chili peppers. With his vegetables, he'd make *salata ghaza-wiya*, a spicy Gazan salad. Pairing the salad with warm *kmaj*, pocket bread that his grandmother would bake, Baba would proceed to *ghammis*—a dipping and scooping maneuver mastered by the Gaza populace.

"So you see, my son, it's in the family," Baba explained. "Your grandfather was a farmer, and your father owned a garden. And your father's vegetables tasted good, not like the food they give us here—stale bread and yogurt that's years past its expiration date. Of course it's not weird that you want to be a farmer. But without education, without knowledge, we are nothing. College is important."

Baba turned to Mohammad and asked him if he'd thought about his future. Yes, Mohammad said; he wanted to study law at Southern Methodist University, and perhaps he'd be granted a soccer scholarship. Upon hearing this, my parents were brimming with pride. I could see in Sami's eyes a wave of frustration, resentment, and guilt. I wanted to say something to him, but before I could do so, Baba turned back to his younger son and said, "Remember what we talked about, all right?"

Sami promised that he would.

For the rest of the visit, we were only interrupted one more time, very briefly, when a guard warned Sami to stop unscrewing the mouthpiece on the receiver.

During the final quarter of the visitation, Mother steered the conversation toward me. She didn't attempt to ease her point into the discussion; she is decisive and direct, an indication that she is indeed the daughter of a retired army general. Mother eats and walks at a rapid pace, which could also be attributed to her father—a stern but loving Palestinian man who told me, during a 2006 visit to Jordan, "Your mother is the most outstanding of all women. You'll never be half the person she is." He said this matter-of-factly, in that way only old people can get away with, after which he kissed my forehead and requested a glass of water.

Now, in the visitation room, Mother turned to me, her eyes a textured emerald, no makeup, her high cheekbones defining her square face and her voice firm and low—a trait that I inherited and loathed during my childhood. She began with simple questions: "What will you do after you graduate? Will you stay in New York?"

"Yes, Mother. I'd like to stay in New York," I said.

"For how long?"

"Not sure. Maybe a few more years."

"If you're done with school, there's no real reason for you to stay. I'd rather you come back to Texas and help me with the boys," she said.

"Mother, I'm not coming back to Texas."

Silence.

"I really don't see myself living in Texas again."

More silence.

"I don't think this is right," she finally said. "What about us? We need you."

"I'll be back to visit, but my life is in New York now."

I looked around for backup, but everyone stayed quiet. Teta pretended like she wasn't listening. Sami, as he customarily does when nervous or bored, was drumming on multiple surfaces.

"Ghassan, talk to your daughter," Mother said.

Baba's eyes welled up.

"Majida, look at our daughter. Noor is a flower. She's almost done with graduate school, and she's become an advocate for her father's innocence. I couldn't be more proud of her."

I had been speaking on campuses across the country about his imprisonment.

Turning to me, he said, "Noor, you are my heart. And because you're so far away, I feel like there's something missing inside me. I don't have a problem with you staying in New York, but I spend all day thinking about you and praying for you and hoping that you stay safe. I just want to suggest one thing, Noor, and I don't want you to be upset; but Noor—my heart—if you can keep your eye out for a partner, someone you think you can spend the rest of your life with, I won't feel so worried. Do you understand?"

I started to pick at my cuticles, a nervous coping mechanism I developed during the court trials. I could only say one thing: "I hate that they're listening."

"I know, I know," Baba said, and after a few Arabic curse words, he continued, "It's ugly what they're doing, and you know I can't do anything about it. But Noor, promise me that you'll at least think about what I said?"

"It's not like I can plan that type of thing."

"Of course you can't, but I'm just saying, don't be so stubborn, and just make an effort. Okay?"

I shrugged.

Baba turned to Mother and said, "Majida, don't be upset. Say something."

"She doesn't care what I think, so why should I say anything?" Mother responded. "She probably wouldn't care if something happened to me tomorrow."

I did care about her, of course. But I was exhausted by her inability to let things go.

Instead of explaining myself, I gently put the receiver back on the hook. Mother shrugged, and she, too, put her phone down. Now Baba was left alone, with no one on the line but himself. He stared at his family. During the previous day, we had been overjoyed by his matless workout; now no one wanted to speak. He looked at us as if saying, Do you want me to leave?

You know when you're in a dream, and you're struggling to say something, anything? A vowel, a grunt? but your voice sounds weak, almost muted? That is how that moment felt.

It's not in Baba's nature to walk away, but on this autumn afternoon, he slid his chair to the door and touched the knob. A way of saying, I can go.

MOMENT STAY

by CATHERINE LACEY

A nurse came in.

Mrs. Riley, Charles is on the phone.

Charles?

Yes. Charles.

She said this like I should absolutely know who Charles was and I could have no possible excuse for not knowing who Charles was and like even the word *Charles* should have carried a very serious meaning for me and I should have already known this meaning and if I did not know what Charles meant there was something severely wrong with me.

Your husband, she said. He's on the phone.

My husband, I said. His name could have been Charles, I thought, yes, I was mostly sure that Charles was the word that people who were not his wife called my husband since they couldn't call him husband since none of them were his wife.

What does Charles say?

He wants to speak with you, she said.

Me?

She just looked this time, annoyed and nothing.

Okay, I said. I'll talk.

So we were having a talk.

We were putting information toward each other and we were doing this as casually as we could pretend to be doing this because it had been a very long time since we had done this and we were out of practice and it was obvious to us, obvious that we were not used to each other, but the main problem I had with this talk was that my husband had put his voice on crookedly—he was wearing it incorrectly, was oriented to it in an ugly way and it hurt to listen to him speak like this in the same way that it hurts to look at someone's bloodied mouth when it is talking and thickened red dribbles out or maybe a tooth— listening to my husband also hurt in the same way that I can barely look at a person with any kind of tumor growing on their face, an ear folded under a puss-filled bulb or a nose swollen into a rubber ball, and this is why it took all the energy I had just to listen to my husband talk in his crooked voice, that voice that sounded wrenched out of his mouth, that voice that sounded like a molar being slowly twisted from gums with the nerves dangling, but

Hello, he said, and How are you, he said, and I said Good, and we knew that wasn't really true and he said I'm good, too, even though it was also obvious he was not good or even close, but regardless of not being good he talked for a while and I made some noises equivalent to an absently nodding head, but after a few minutes of this he asked, Are you even listening to me? It's been months and can't you even listen to me? Is it so much to ask you just to fucking listen to me for once? and I knew listening to him was important, so I tried my best to listen, to take his words in and fold them in the correct fashion, to make a smooth warm stack of his words, a just-laundered white socks and white towels kind of stack, a bleached and tumble-dried stack that I could look at and say, yes, I had completed this chore, this thing in life that needed doing: hearing my husband's complaints, his current ones. I told my husband, It's just a lot, to listen—to hear you right now. I am—I am overwhelmed, a little. I am a little overwhelmed. And my husband said, Yes, I understand that, but I don't think he really did understand that or even that it could be understood, what my life was like at that point and why it was overwhelming me. The moss green hospital room and the locked door and a person from the embassy telling me I was illegal, in a way, and Mrs. Harper telling me they needed to psychologically assess me and that little painting of the man who owned the ocean hanging over there on that wall, that little smug man reminding me that I didn't own anything right then, not even the freedom I'd once had and not even a glass of ocean water. All I had was my husband's voice asking if I was being treated well, if the immigration officers were being fair and decent and if the nurses and doctors were being kind and polite and I wanted

to answer him with something true, to tell him something
specific so he would know that I was listening and
answering, making a real effort, and as I thought of what to
say I looked through the narrow window in the locked door
and saw a nurse put her hand on her lower back and twist
so slightly to the right and the way she did this reminded
me of the bartender on the ferry from Picton to Wellington
and how the tender tender had been so very tender in the
way she had slid cold pints into everyone's hands and her
movements—pulling on the taps, turning on tiptoe back
toward me, the straight-backed grace she had even as she
leaned down to rest her head in her beer-wet hands—even
those little things were tender things and I thought of how
the tender tender had treated me or, rather, the possible
world that she had suggested just by existing the way that
she had, the possible life she had hinted toward with her
grace, and I thought, then in the hospital, that there was a
glimmer of the tender tender in the nurse as she pressed her
spread fingers against her back and because of this balmy
memory I felt a passing niceness and I told my husband
they were treating me very well at the hospital, that
everyone here was being professional and graceful and kind
though, in fact, no one had really treated me at all and
I had only spoken to that nurse with the phone and Mrs.
Harper, who hadn't had too much grace or kindness but at
least had seemed, in a way, professional, since her profession
seemed to be to make people aware of the bad things that
they had done. The way that the rest of the people at the
hospital hadn't yet treated me was not unkind, and there
was still a potential for everyone to be sweet and polite and
professional, since there had been no evidence, yet, of
anyone being the exact opposite of those things—so I told

my husband that I was fine and he apologized for having to
make me go through all this, but said it had seemed to him
that this would be the only way for anything to work out,
that telling the embassy that I was a risk to myself and
others was really the only thing that was going to motivate
them to look for me, and he knew, he said, that I needed to
be found, that I wasn't, for whatever reason, really within
myself anymore but on the phone he still said, I know
you're not a risk to yourself or others, Elly, I know that
you're not, you know—dangerous—you know that, right?
That is what he asked me: if I knew that he thought
I wasn't a risk to myself or others, which, I believed,
overlooked the fact that I had been escorted by two cops to
a hospital where I was locked in a small green room and an
immigration officer had come to tell me that I had violated
laws and that I was, in general, a bad or at least highly
suspect person and that I would need to be mentally and
emotionally assessed, that an inventory needed to be taken
because they weren't entirely sure if everything I was
supposed to have in me was still in me, and all this was
basically telling me in many ways that I was, in fact, a risk
of some sort, that there was a part of my life or the lives of
others that I had been putting at risk because cops don't go
carting un-risky people to hospitals and immigration
officers don't go locking un-risky people into hospital
rooms, and these are not the things we do to people who
are not a risk to something, Husband, I thought but did
not say. I was a risk. And my husband knew that and he
also knew that I knew that. I did not want to admit this
then but I can admit it now and will: I wanted to be
responsible for destroying a small to medium-size part
of my husband. And this was a somewhat-sick and

somewhat-normal thing, I think: everyone really just wants to feel like they could destroy a part of someone who loves them, though not everyone can see that ugly want sleeping under the blankets of love and affection and secure attachment that we try to smother that ugly want with and even fewer people will really allow that want to become an action, to take any kind of pleasure in seeing the destroying done. Everyone has an ugly want to be needed so badly that if we were to withhold ourselves from that person who needs us so, we would leave them so empty of their need they'd become completely irrelevant to the world, unable to go on in a normal, functional, just fine, forward-moving fashion. The short of it is this: my husband was a mess, and even though I knew I was also a mess, I also knew he was messier, at least in some ways, and I no longer had any interest in taking responsibility for him, the crumple and grunt of him, my husband, this life I had welded myself to—he and the way he was and the way he wanted me to be. While I was thinking of this my husband was saying something to me about the choices I had made but I already knew that I had made a poor choice or series of choices. My choices were poor, they were broke, they were bankrupt of all value to other people. My choices were only of any value to me and that value, I was coming to find, was also highly debatable, now that I was sitting stiff and still dressed on a hospital bed, waiting for someone to come fully analyze my internal, unseeable being, knowing so certainly they would just say what I already knew—that there had been no discernible or obvious reason behind anything that I had done, leaving my husband without a word and wandering this country for so long. I was just out here, all huddled in my nothing. I could only explain all my poor choices by saying that I had a general feeling of needing to constantly leave, of needing to be the first to go, of needing to barricade myself from living life the way everyone else seemed to be living it, the way that seemed obvious to them or intuitive or clear or easy—easy to everyone who was on the other side of this place called I.

Nothing is clear or easy to me anymore, I said to my husband, quietly, and he told me, still in that malformed voice, that he had something very important to tell me. He said he would leave a letter with the doorman of his (not our) building, and that letter would tell me what I was supposed to do. This letter would outline what remained of the life I'd left, and what of it I could still claim. He breathed in and balanced his voice on what seemed to be the last stable edge of himself.

Elly, I am not yet sure what to do with you or myself, if there is still a context in which we can exist. You have complicated all the general contexts in which we had formerly existed, Elyria, you have tested their outer reaches. There are limits to what a man can stand, to how much being treated unlike a husband he can take before he is, in fact, no longer a husband, no longer willing to be the half of the life that he had thought he was living in.

I was listening to him as carefully as I could, still taking his words into my hands and folding them into smooth rectangles and putting them in a neat stack beside me. I was still doing this chore and I found another little stack of comfort when my husband told me what my next step would be, that after I was sent back to New York there would be this letter and that seemed nice, having

a letter with instructions, directions, maybe even a list
with open boxes for checking beside and I could go check,
check, check, done, done, done and be back in my life or
its vague approximation. After he told me about the letter
he said that he couldn't talk anymore because he needed to
go, but it was clear in the way that he spoke that he didn't
really need to, he just wanted to, though I may not be the
kind of person who can be relied upon to make a distinc-
tion between wants and needs, and I may not be a person
who can parse any space between needing and wanting or
even wanting and being compelled or being compelled
and being swallowed whole by something, picked up and
taken away by something like a desire, something like a
need, something like a compulsion. But I knew what my
husband really meant when he said that he needed to go
was that he wanted to hang up the phone and pour himself a glass of gin if the hour was appropriate or even if the
hour was inappropriate and he wanted to go sit in his chair,
his favorite chair—the beige one with the stain on the left
arm—and he wanted to put on a record, one of his mother's
records, that unlabeled one that he'd never heard when he
was a child but it was still one that she had owned, had
probably paid money for or was given at some point, this
recording of a string quartet performing something just
morose enough for everyday listening, and the composer
had always been unknown because the tune was unfamiliar
and the original sleeve had been lost and replaced by a fold
of plain cardboard, and as he sat in his chair and listened
to this record for the thousandth time and as he held his
first glass of gin, he would keep the tempo of the quartet
by swinging his head so slightly to the right (with his eyes
closed) then back to center then throw his chin up (still

with his eyes closed) then back to center and to the right
again, center, and up again, center, eyes closed and right,
center, and up, center, still with shut eyes and right, center,
up, center and he would do this for hours, eyes always
closed, as the record played and ended, and he'd turn it to
the B side then to the A side again and the B and the A
and this, I knew, was what he really meant by, I need to
go, Elyria; he meant he had to go into the place that he
went when I became too much for him, the place where
he conducted music played by men or women who were
(maybe) long since dead, men or women whom he'd only
known as violins, a viola, a cello, men or women who had
therefore, essentially, always been dead to him, alive only
in the recorded shadow of once vibrating strings, alive only
when the record spun, but somehow his mother was in that
record, I knew, and that's why he had to play it, that's why
he had to conduct it, that's why he had to be a conductor
to that music, that energy, her energy, that last crackly,
rotating bit of his mother that existed and my husband
conducted those songs, also, because I was too much for him
to conduct and for that I would like to apologize, that I had
always been the wrong watt for my husband, that I was
always tripping his circuit, that I was never something he
could quite carry.

The nurse took the cordless phone out of my hand
and walked out without any kind of explanation. The
door audibly locked behind her and I was left with myself
behind that locked door and even though this wasn't
a particularly nice place that I was in—a small room
painted a color that was the same color as a certain color
of mold—I decided or perhaps just felt then that I wanted
for this exact moment to stay a while longer than any other

moment. I said to myself Moment, you should stay, you
should stay even though I know you can't and wouldn't
even if you could, and I wanted this, I now realize, because
I loved the limits I had in that moment, the ugly limits I had—the edges of my hospital bed and the hideous
walls of that room and the door and the lock in the door
and the country that was keeping me and the observations
that were being made about me and the knowledge that
a psychiatrist and his attendants were on their way, were
steadily marching toward me, that they were going to ask
me questions and record my answers and their own observations, they were going to watch how my eyes moved and
when and watch where I put my hands and how, and all
these little things were going to be recorded, flattened out
onto a sheet of paper that would tell the embassy and the
immigration agents and Homeland Security and my waiting husband exactly what I was and why I was what I was,
and I loved that these were the cozy limits of my little
life, in the limit of this moment, in the antiseptic huddle
of the hospital room—well, I wanted it to stay, just like
that April day, the first spring since Ruby had split herself
open on the brick courtyard, and the first spring since I had
met the professor who would become my husband, when
he and I were in a park, lying on a quilt he told me his
mother had made and for the first time since meeting him
he smiled when he talked of his mother, and the professor
and I were in the park and lying on our sides on the quilt
and holding hands and looking in each other's eyes and
each of our hearts were making themselves known to us as
highly functional organs—beating like the strongest and
most patriotic of soldiers leading the march of our little
lives—and so the professor and I were the most in love

that two people could ever be because we were united by
a common, gristly loss and despite this or because of this
we had allowed ourselves to fall in love during that all-
time darkest autumn, but then later, after the snow had
come and had gone and the ground had dried and trees
had leaves again and here we were in the middle of it all,
staring at the impossibility of spring, again it was spring,
and at the impossibility of being so alive and being so
awake with someone else and the professor, staring at me
in this yellow moment, decided to say something someone
long dead had said or written: he said, Moment stay, and
I said, What? and he said, It's something Virginia Woolf
wrote: Moment stay because you are so fair, or something
like that, and I said, So this is how you feel? How Virginia
Woolf already felt? and he said, Yes, and what I felt then was
partially agreement with him because, yes, I was also in love
and wanted to stay in it, but also a kind of sadness, a kind of
anger, a kind of disappointment, because as soon as he had
asked that moment to stay, it was gone.

ZERO HOUR

THE COVERT STRUGGLE FOR TRIPOLI
AND THE FUTURE OF LIBYA

nonfiction by WILLIAM WHEELER

A t 3 p.m. on August 20, 2011, a black Honda SUV carrying four men pulled to a stop outside a row of unfinished town houses in a residential section of Tripoli. About a dozen guards were scattered around the empty complex, keeping watch. They recognized Mohammed Gizawi, a lieutenant colonel in the Libyan air force, and allowed their visitors to pass. Gizawi's uncle, fifty-seven-year-old Nagmi Rayes, a one-time officer in the Libyan army, led the way inside, through the doorless entrance of a two-story villa paneled with drywall. They were headed for the operations room of what they hoped would be the endgame of the Libyan revolution.

Life in the capital had by then become the stuff of
nightmares. From behind the fortified walls of his compound, Muammar Qaddafi had vowed to hunt down his
opponents and cleanse the city "inch by inch, house by
house, room by room, alley by alley." There were wide-
spread rumors, accepted as fact, that the regime had planted
bombs throughout the sewer system. Security forces were
conducting nightly raids, arresting anyone suspected of
activism, and distributing weapons to their supporters
ahead of an expected rebel assault. "Every individual will be
armed," Qaddafi had announced. "Libya will become a hell."

Rayes and his allies, meanwhile, had been working in
secret to hasten the dictator's demise, preparing a covert
operation to take control of the city from within. Among
them were senior military and security officials, lawyers and
businessmen, and even a few members of Qaddafi's inner
circle. The day before his visit to the town houses, Rayes
had called Mahmoud Shammam, an official in the rebel
government based in Benghazi, to ask if the moment to act
had arrived. Rayes's group functioned autonomously, but
Shammam served as their liaison to NATO and the rebel
forces approaching Tripoli from the mountains. Now Rayes
was supposed to call back in an hour to learn whether the
men Shammam represented were on board.

Inside the villa, Rayes found Mohammed Sheikh—
a bald, gray-bearded man of fifty-four who was their group's
leader by default. Sheikh had left his hideout on a friend's
farm ninety minutes before, and was leaning over a printer,
watching the progress of a letter he had just written to the
leaders of all eighty-nine of Tripoli's underground cells,
announcing the start of Zero Hour at 8 p.m. that night.
Sheikh greeted his guests calmly, and told them he had

made up his mind to proceed. Rayes asked him to wait until they heard back from Shammam.

Sheikh declined. "We're going out tonight," he said.

Nagmi Rayes joined the army in 1977, not out of love for Qaddafi but a need for self-preservation: soldiers had questioned his father about why his sons were being educated abroad instead of serving their country. At the time, Rayes's family owned properties all over Tripoli, including the city's largest carpet market; Qaddafi confiscated it the next year as part of a sweeping economic reform. "He took everything from us," Rayes told me in September 2011.

Since not long after Qaddafi first struck out at protesters, Rayes had been working with his own small cell—his brother Naser, his nephew, and a few friends—to find ways to weaken the regime and prepare for Tripoli's liberation. In May, a childhood friend, Sadat Elbadri, had linked him up to an umbrella resistance group called the Coalition of February 17, which had been absorbing more and more local cells throughout the spring. By that time, the Tripoli rebels had a military council headed by a former army officer, Mustafa Noah, and were fundraising to buy weapons, plan small attacks, and undermine the military. "Everybody was looking for a group to join," said Rayes. Tripoli was ripe with discontent, and it was not hard to find would-be rebels among the frustrated professionals, disaffected military officers, and young men looking for work—two generations exasperated with the failures and eccentricities of Qaddafi's bizarre misrule.

Rayes's friend Elbadri had spent most of his life abroad; as part of the National Front for the Salvation of Libya, he had worked for more than a decade to bring down Qaddafi. After so much fruitless struggle, he saw the Arab Spring as the opening he had been waiting for. In the wake of the successful revolutions in Egypt and Tunisia, he told his old friends that "50 percent of our job has been done."

The relatively peaceful protests elsewhere may have been enough to topple dictators like Mubarak and Ben Ali, who were slow to grasp the scale of the threats they faced. But Qaddafi's response to the initial discontent was quick and unrelenting, and Rayes was convinced that the man would never give up power peacefully. After security forces opened fire on unarmed Tripoli protesters in late February, Rayes decided that violent confrontation was "the right way," he said. "To go out in the street and shout and be killed every day—that's wrong."

Ultimately, their coalition grew to comprise the aforementioned eighty-nine separate cells. The rebels were arranged like a bunch of grapes, Mohammed Sheikh said later, with the men at the bottom connected only indirectly to those at the top. The leader of each cell was responsible for organizing and arming his own group. Most of the rebels involved knew their comrades in other cells, if at all, only by code name.

Many of their supporters were men like Rayes's brother—liberal capitalists who wanted to be able to vote, use the internet, and do business without being considered the laughingstock of the international community. Naser Rayes owned an IT company; he had studied in the U.S. and the UK, and knew life outside Qaddafi's rule. Now he was one of many white-collar professionals passing information to the rebels. When we first met, in early September, as celebratory machine gun fire rang out from Tripoli's newly liberated streets, he was sipping a screwdriver made with vodka smuggled in from Tunisia in a water bottle. I asked if he thought alcohol would be legal in the new Libya. "Hopefully," he said. "But there are too many religious people around."

We were seated at a table in his "bachelor's pad"—a modestly sized third-floor abode that accommodated a sofa and lounge chair, a pile of Kiss albums, an electronic drum kit, a treadmill, and, poking out from under a red blanket in the corner, a pile of assault rifles. Across the room was his home entertainment center, which contained a secret compartment that housed the satellite receiver he'd used to communicate with his fellow conspirators after the regime shut down the internet.

Naser explained to me that many of them had simply been fed up with business as usual in Qaddafi's Libya: the lack of decent schools, the systemic corruption, the fear of offending another driver in traffic who might turn out to be a security agent who could pull you from your car and beat you in the street. The situation was even bleaker for the younger generation, trapped without the access to education that Naser had enjoyed; before the uprising, unemployment estimates ran as high as 30 percent. Naser saw the revolution as the only chance to leave behind a better Libya for his kids.

And so, as spring continued, Naser gathered coordinates of weapons caches to be bombed, transcripts of phone conversations, and the names and passport numbers of suspected foreign mercenaries—mostly men from Chad, Niger, and Mali—from his contacts in the government. He began sending along the information to Libyan expats, who would in turn relay it to NATO, to allies in Qatar, or to the rebel government in Benghazi. Meanwhile Nagmi, his brother, began looking for guns.

In March, a NATO intervention staved off what many feared would be a bloodbath in Benghazi. Loyalist tanks had pushed up to the outskirts of the city when French jets and American cruise missiles swooped in, allowing rebels to reclaim lost ground and saving the city. Around this time, back in Tripoli, the Rayeses' brother-in-law, a high-ranking military official named Hussein Nayed, agreed to help them gather arms against the regime.

Nayed wrote a special permit that allowed Nagmi to take weapons directly from the military, ostensibly to defend the city from rebels. Starting in late March, Nagmi made several trips to an army base to retrieve Kalashnikovs—a handful at a time to avoid arousing suspicion, until he'd collected about three dozen rifles in all. He acquired another two dozen from two other military friends, army generals. By then the Libyan ranks were filled with men of divided loyalties.

In early April, Nagmi traveled to the Tunisian resort town of Djerba in order to link up with another opposition group. A mutual friend set up a late-night meeting for him in a coffee shop; when he showed up, he realized he already knew two of the three men waiting for him from his social circle back home. Rayes explained to them that he had a good connection inside the regime, and was gathering arms. They talked awhile, and then the men told him he would be contacted with further instructions.

A few hours later, he got a call giving him directions to a Djerba hotel. There he spent more than two hours talking with Hisham Buhagiar, a rebel colonel who had lived in the U.S. and trained with special-forces units in Iraq and Sudan. Buhagiar had been dispatched from Tripoli by the February 17 coalition to train fighters for an eventual uprising. He had since sent some two dozen Tripoli residents to the arid Nafusah mountains, just across the border in western Libya, where they were being trained to use electronic-targeting devices that would be planted around the capital to help NATO bombers hit a list of suggested targets without killing bystanders.

This was the plan that the National Transitional Council, as the rebels' shadow government was called, had been peddling to NATO officials and French president Nicolas Sarkozy. The rebels had been steadily collecting information from men like the Rayeses, and they were counting on local resistance groups to support their forces when they stormed the city. (Their plan would eventually involve the help of General Barrani Ishkal, Qaddafi's cousin, who was in charge of a well-armed battalion guarding Tripoli's entrance, and who was then concluding a secret agreement with the rebels. Individual fighters slipped discreetly into the city, aided by U.S. Predator drone surveillance and training, weapons, and financing from Qatar, the United Arab Emirates, France, Italy, and the UK, but Ishkal let the main force in.) Nagmi believed that they would need to work together or risk a bloodbath.

He joined up with the Tripoli coalition shortly afterward. There, the rebels divvied up assignments among those with the right skills or contacts to get each job done: fundraising, smuggling weapons, blowing up the cars of security personnel, attacking checkpoints with blast-fishing dynamite tossed from the back of a motorcycle. But the central function of their larger coalition was to decide when to pull the trigger on a citywide show of resistance.

The plan was straightforward: when the signal was given, all rebel cells would lock down their neighborhoods, ensuring that the locals stayed out of their cars. Then they would shoot at any vehicle that tried to enter their territory, leaving the government troops with nowhere to run when the main rebel force arrived. By shutting down traffic, the rebels would force their opponents to move slowly on foot, through unfamiliar streets, making them easier to pick off. Here their compartmentalized cell structure would be an asset—small, organically formed groups, whose members knew and trusted each other, would be fighting for their own communities under the eyes of their families and neighbors.

The first Zero Hour was set for June 18. A barrage of NATO air strikes had failed to dislodge Qaddafi from his compound, and the rebel army, a ragtag assembly of regional militias, was struggling to advance. It had become clear that if Tripoli were to fall, it would take a popular uprising from within.

But the regime soon got wind of the plan. The Rayeses' brother-in-law, Hussein, came out of a top-level security meeting and warned Nagmi to "tell everybody who is going out to take their coffins with them, because they're going to die." They had lost the element of surprise, so they postponed their plans for another month.

Meanwhile, the conspirators tried to maintain their double lives. The regime was rumored to have cars that could monitor phone conversations roving the city, and security agents were bursting into homes to conduct impromptu searches. One day in June, Naser got a call from a friend telling him that one of his allies had been arrested at 2 a.m. the night before; the police had taken the man's computers and cell phones, as well. Naser panicked. His brother told him to disconnect every bit of equipment he'd used and get ready to run; Naser shut down his internet connection and hid the satellite phones he had smuggled in from Tunisia, expecting he would be arrested at any minute. It was only after two dreadful days of waiting that Naser's friend, Waheb Alwalda, resurfaced—savagely beaten, but alive.

Alwalda had survived because he was smart and well connected. He had been beaten for four hours before the authorities checked his phone, which contained the names and numbers of several influential members of the regime. The agents contacted them, and they vouched for Alwalda; his friends, meanwhile, swamped the station with calls on his behalf. Alwalda held out, professing his love for Qaddafi, admitting nothing. After two days, they let him go. Four days later, he went back to the detention center to make friends with his former guards, and begin extracting information from them.

Late in June, Mohammed Gizawi, the Rayeses' nephew, introduced his friend Hisham Elhekti to Nagmi. Elhekti, a lieutenant colonel in the army, had been tapped by his mosque's imam to lead the resistance in his neighborhood. He had a PhD in radar technology, but he knew he lacked the expertise to plan an urban combat mission. He was looking for a mentor in the preparation for revolution. Nagmi, who was well-known in military circles from his days teaching at the infantry academy, fit the bill.

It turned out that both Elhekti and Rayes had acquired Kalashnikovs from the same source: a general who had helped Qaddafi seize power in 1969, and who had recently been faking an illness to avoid a summons to Algeria to help plan the counterrevolution. Elhekti was a neighbor and a relative of the general, and had obtained his tacit support and twenty Kalashnikovs. That wouldn't be enough. Their neighborhood was nearby Bab al Aziziya, the compound where Qaddafi had resettled his die-hard supporters, and where the dictator himself lived under the protection of his personal guard. Any action there would not go unopposed.

So like most of those looking for weapons in Tripoli, Elhekti had to buy them. He had collected €200,000 in all, largely from sympathetic businessmen. (His younger brother brought half of it—from allies in Qatar—across the Tunisian border in five-hundred-euro notes stashed in various pockets.) A few weeks earlier, Elhekti explained to Rayes when they first met, a friend had introduced him to a lawyer who lived outside the capital. The man was transporting AK-47s and rocket launchers, purchased from soldiers and smugglers in the loyalist stronghold of Bani Walid, into the city via an extremely circuitous, roadblock-avoiding route. In a cell phone video the lawyer showed me later, you can see him stripping his Peugeot 206 of its cargo in Elhekti's garage, pulling pistols, grenades, and brown paper cubes of ammunition out of the dashboard.

At a subsequent meeting in his home, Rayes introduced Elhekti to Sadat Elbadri and others from his circle. The men were meeting with their own cells almost every day, and

Rayes had convened the gathering to give them the latest information from his brother-in-law about the regime's weapons caches and operations centers. By that time, loyalty within the army's ranks was rapidly withering.

What he did not share was his growing concern that the rebels outside the city were only reluctantly coordinating their efforts with the Tripoli cells. During his last visit to Djerba, in mid-July, he had reiterated to Buhagiar that his men were eager to act. The colonel had said that NATO needed more time to bomb, and urged Rayes to hold off for another week or so. Rayes agreed, but suspected that Buhagiar's men were mainly interested in riding in like cowboys to save the day. In the last month, rebel forces had taken large areas of the Nafusah mountains, gaining a foothold in the loyalist-controlled west and their closest frontline yet to the capital; now fighters there were telling reporters they would take Tripoli by late August.

Rayes didn't believe they could pull that off alone. And, even if they could, why should they? After they had lived so long under Qaddafi's shadow, the revolution was a chance for Tripoli's people to show their courage, just as every other free city had done. If they did not, Rayes feared they would be remembered as "slaves."

The Tripoli coalition's military wing was moving forward with its own plans. When they received word of a secret government-intelligence meeting at a Tripoli hotel, one that Qaddafi's son Seif al-Islam and his brother-in-law Abdullah Senussi were set to attend, they decided to plan an attack. Hussein Nayed supplied $15,000 in cash to secure getaway cars and an RPG.

In the event, the rockets meant for the meeting missed, striking a wall and the roof of the hotel. Mohammed Sheikh would later say they counted the mission as a success, of sorts, because in the aftermath of the attack they had been able to confirm that their targets had in fact been there. It showed their intelligence was solid.

But the cell soon faced a more critical setback. In late July, one of their men was arrested at the Tunisian border; five others were picked up almost simultaneously, including Mustafa Noah, still the head of their military council. Sheikh decided that someone must have talked. Suddenly the rest of their leaders were on the run, with some crossing into Tunisia through the mountains.

It could have been a debilitating turn of events. But rather than run, Mohammed Sheikh and one of his comrades, army general Wanis Sahli, decided to remain in Tripoli. They checked into a hotel that evening, then traveled early the next morning to a friend's farm on the outskirts of the city to hide out. Security theory, as Sheikh describes it, says that the first forty-eight hours after your name shows up on a wanted list are the most crucial. After that, you slide further down the list of targets, as newly wanted figures assume priority. They let slip rumors that they had fled to Tunisia. Sheikh used a courier to coordinate the deception from his hideout on the farm.

He described it as the best period of his life. A month felt like a lifetime because he lived so intensely, alternating between fear and calm, buoyed by an unflagging sense of purpose. General Sahli was a source of reassurance, reminding his companion that their struggle would help bring about a better future for Libya. The food they ate, which was cooked on wood-fired stoves by women they didn't know, tasted better than anything Sheikh had ever eaten at Tripoli's finest hotels.

Every few days, Nagmi Rayes would visit to discuss their plans. Because many of their allies still held positions of power within the official security apparatus, they had excellent intelligence on what the regime was doing. They even managed to freeze official funds. In the last days before the uprising, according to Sheikh, a top-ranking general loyal to Qaddafi tried to withdraw about 75 million dollars from an official account. But the signature of one of their cell's members, a colonel, was required for such withdrawals. He didn't sign, and the general left the bank empty-handed.

In mid-August, the capital's rebels held their largest meeting, on the farm of a co-conspirator. They worried about spies infiltrating the gathering, so attendance was limited to about two dozen of their most trusted leaders. All the neighborhoods of Tripoli were represented, from the western port of Janzour to the eastern edge of Tajura. Many of the men there that day felt they weren't ready for action; the balance of troops, guns, and munitions still heavily favored the regime. Not even Sheikh could say with certainty how many people were behind them. They had gathered weapons for around three thousand fighters, but how many they could count on when the fighting began was an open question. They knew there were others waiting to take up arms, and many believed their neighbors would be inspired to join them in the fight. But they would only have one opportunity to get it right.

Others at the meeting, though, were anxious for combat, and the timing looked good. After six months of deadlock—with the rebels holding primarily the eastern cities, and Qaddafi holding most of the west—rebels backed by critical NATO airpower had in recent weeks made a dramatic push toward Tripoli from the western mountains, inspiring similar drives from the south and east. The loyalists were now fighting on multiple fronts, stretching their forces thin. August 20, meanwhile, had long been discussed as a fortuitous date to mobilize popular support, because it marked the anniversary of the day the Prophet Mohammed had captured Mecca. If they delayed much longer, they would miss Ramadan—the holy month that gave them a window in the evening to strike, while people were off the streets, breaking the fast with their families. The most persuasive argument came from the rebels in Souq Juma, a neighborhood that had witnessed nightly skirmishes between rebel groups and security forces. They were tired of watching idly as the government swooped up their friends in raids during the night, and worried that if they didn't move soon, they would never get the chance.

The rebels had another reason for haste, as well: a source in Qaddafi's intelligence network had warned them of plans to execute one thousand prisoners at Abu Salim prison on September 1. And although they did not yet know it, intelligence chief Abdullah Senussi was personally overseeing the torture and interrogation of two of their co-conspirators within Abu Salim, and demanding to know the whereabouts of Sheikh and Sahli.

On August 19, Nagmi Rayes, fed up with waiting for word from the operations room in Djerba, called his contact there and was given the number for NTC spokesman Mahmoud Shammam. Shammam said he would need to talk with the rebels in the mountains. He told Rayes to call back at 4 p.m. the next day. Mohammed Sheikh and General Sahli told Rayes to come by an hour before that, so they could give him their own decision about whether they would go out that night.

The whole city was on edge. The Rayeses were continuing to monitor the government security forces' discussions: "It was shoot first, ask questions later," Naser recalled. They later discovered supplies of whiskey and what they believed to be amphetamines that Qaddafi had laid in for his fighters. On August 19, they overheard radio chatter that sounded like something out of the Rwandan genocide. It was the voice of a security agent spurring his men to battle: "Kill, kill, this is your time. This is your time for victory. Destroy the rats."

At 4 p.m. on August 20, after his meeting with Mohammed Sheikh, Nagmi Rayes returned to his brother's house, which had been designated as the backup operations room in case security forces destroyed the villa. He parked out front and called Shammam. It was a short conversation. Shammam informed him that the rebels from the mountains would, indeed, be coming to Tripoli that night; they would arrive by 11 p.m. "We're going out tonight at eight," Rayes told him. "We're not going to wait for anyone." Shammam wished him good luck, and they hung up.

Over the next few hours, Nagmi crisscrossed the city: he swung by his office for extra ammunition, to his father's house to tell a friend that he should bring men to Nagmi's house at eight o'clock, to Hussein Nayed's house to pick up an extra fifteen rifles. His brother-in-law had just come out of a meeting in Qaddafi's operations room, and confirmed that the regime knew nothing of their plans that night.

Meanwhile, Mohammed Gizawi, now the designated

courier for Rayes's cell, had agreed to deliver to several other cells their copy of the official Zero Hour letter, which contained instructions to secure their neighborhoods and to treat captives humanely, giving them food and water and medical attention, and also called on doctors to treat the injured and on local families to feed the rebels.

Gizawi's route took him through a city that was already under siege, its supply lines cut by recent rebel gains. NATO strikes had pummeled Qaddafi's compound and the home of Abdullah Senussi earlier in the week, and some residents had fled the city. Food and power were in short supply, uncollected garbage had piled up in the streets, and two more of the regime's top officials had defected. For months, those in the military had had to keep showing up at their jobs or risk being called out as traitors, but as the gas shortages intensified throughout the summer, everyone else had stopped going to work more than a few times a month. A few days earlier, Gizawi had told his commanding officer, a friend who had already declared to him that they should join the rebels when they arrived, that he would soon be taking up arms against the regime. The man told Gizawi to "go with the blessings of God."

By then, the fall of Qaddafi seemed inevitable; the question was how many would have to die for it to happen. As an ominous precedent, Gizawi had the images from Misrata, Libya's third-largest city, which had been the scene of months of house-to-house fighting: torched homes sprayed with gunfire, sixth-floor apartments gutted by artillery, whole corners of buildings blasted away. This was the fate he felt he was working to prevent.

Around 6 p.m., Gizawi pulled up to the Ben Nabi mosque in quiet, tree-shaded Mansura, Hisham Elhekti's neighborhood, which was wedged between downtown Tripoli and the Qaddafi bastion of Bab al Aziziya. Elhekti, who had been waiting eagerly for word there all day, was in a meeting with men from a resistance group in an adjacent neighborhood, trying to convince them to join the fight when the time came. He seized on the letter from Gizawi as a semblance of officialdom, proof they were not alone and that others would be coming out with them. "We're working with all of Tripoli," he said, passing the letter around for the others to see.

The mosque was Elhekti's base and his armory. Hidden in a half-full water tank out back were the weapons he had gathered: assault rifles, machine guns, RPGs, and pipe bombs made with gunpowder from anti-aircraft shells. The imam, Abdulrazaq Mshereb, a longtime member of the opposition, had for months walked a dangerous line. Saadi Qaddafi, the dictator's third son, who was remodeling his two-story home in the neighborhood, would occasionally drop by to chat with the imam, even as the man was burying arms on the mosque grounds to use against Saadi's father. The imam spoke in Friday sermons about the people's responsibility to defeat "the enemy." Any intelligence agents in the congregation could interpret his words as denouncing the rebels. But those who knew him understood who the real enemy was: he had a house just down the street.

Nagmi Rayes pulled up to his own house around five minutes to eight. A few of the neighborhood guys were loitering on the corner, as they had done each night for months; many already had their own guns. The father of one had called Rayes a few weeks prior, asking him to give his son some training. Worried they would act too early on their own, Rayes had agreed, but he had made the men promise to wait to reveal themselves until he gave the word. Now, he told them to get their friends, eat something quick, and hurry over to his house.

Rayes's home was soon filled with three dozen college-age kids, so crowded he had trouble finding a spot to change into his heavy-duty cargo pants. The sight of so many young men gathered in his living room that night—kids who had answered his call at a moment's notice, the same kids with the sagging pants whose generation Rayes had always thought indolent—filled him with pride. Their rallying cry was the Takbir, the cry of "Allah Hu Akbar"—"God is Great"—that can be used to signal distress, celebration, determination, or defiance. It would give the people of Tripoli needed courage.

The stakes were clear. As the graffiti scrawled on walls in other Libyan cities proclaimed, they would "win or die." But as they moved out, Rayes was preoccupied by a sense of responsibility for the young men he was leading. His own son was among them, a skinny twenty-year-old who appears in a photo taken that night with a kaffiyeh wrapped around his head and a look in his eye that says he would *not* be waiting out the revolution from the sidelines. Rayes hadn't even told his wife what he was doing, let alone that he would be taking her child into battle. But what could he do—tell his son that he was not yet a man, when even younger boys were going out with them that night? He moved into the streets focused on killing the driver of any vehicle that crossed his sights.

* * *

Around 8 p.m., Elhekti met his imam at the mosque for a last prayer. Then he went home to tell his wife he was about to help launch the battle for Tripoli. He had kept her in the dark for months. "Women like to speak," he explained later. A military man, he was used to keeping secrets. But his family had known he was up to something; a few weeks earlier, his mother caught him unloading boxes of ammo from the garage. When she asked what he was doing, he lied to her, saying the boxes contained computer printers.

When, at last, Elhekti confessed to his wife—telling her that he had been working to bring the revolution to Tripoli, that it was about to begin, and that he would be leading the resistance in their neighborhood that very night—she began to weep. She pleaded with him to stay home and keep safe. But when he told her it was his patriotic duty to help bring down the government, she collected herself and told her husband that God would help him in his cause.

The temperature was in the eighties as Elhekti left his house, wearing a heavy pair of gray cargo pants, a blue denim shirt, and safety boots—gear his brother had bought to sell to oil companies, but that Elhekti figured would make good battle attire. The plan was that Mansura would be the last cell activated; because the army was so heavily concentrated there, the rebels in Elhekti's area would wait for the troops to fan out around the city before attempting to take control of their own streets. They would hold back until 9:30, then launch a strike on a nearby army post, where they hoped to find weapons and free any prisoners.

But when cries of Allah Hu Akbar began to resound

from nearby mosques, Elhekti and the imam decided that security forces would be coming at them soon enough anyway. They worried that they would be captured, and that their own chapter of the revolution would be over before it began. So Elhekti drove his black Toyota Camry out into the middle of the street and parked it in front of the mosque. Then he moved a large work truck to block off the intersection. When his friend Abdulwahab Almgairbi, a stout, cheerful twenty-nine-year-old whose home had been transformed into an emergency field hospital, saw him striding through the street—with a Kalashnikov in one hand and his satellite phone in the other—he thought Elhekti was jacked up on adrenaline, overeager and screwing up the plan. But the sight of his friend out in the open with a weapon struck Almgairbi as the "cardinal sign of revolution." He recognized the point of no return, and went to get his own rifle.

At the mosque, they began distributing Kalashnikovs to the two dozen men who had trickled in early for prayers. They were handing up weapons from within the water tank when a car pulled onto the street and parked behind Elhekti's Camry. Two men emerged and started toward the mosque. Startled, Almgairbi thrust his rifle over the top of the wall, firing blindly in their direction; the men ran off, scattering into the night. Elhekti began posting his recruits in defensive positions around the mosque and the perimeter of the neighborhood, in spots he had marked off on an image from Google Earth. He feared he would have too much blood on his hands if he put them into attack formations. Elhekti had chosen not to conduct military training for his neighbors, afraid it would attract too much attention—a mistake, he now decided. A few hours earlier, one of his fighters had asked him how to shoot a gun.

When the Takbir began, people started running to the mosque, anxious to find out what was wrong. The imam, struggling against habit, reluctantly told them there would be no prayers that evening. The women should return to their homes, he said, and the men should stay and fight.

In Nagmi Rayes's neighborhood, his men had started by locking down their zone, moving whatever they could find—mostly piles of wood, large rocks, and other building materials from a mosque under construction—to close off the streets. Nagmi had prepared a list of the likely Qaddafi supporters nearby, and now he went to a handful of homes to disarm them, telling the men that if they remained inside they would not be harmed.

From the rooftop deck outside his operations room, Naser Rayes and his friend Alwalda listened to the security forces' radio calls on a scanner. They could hear the first shots being fired in Souq Juma, where the rebels had taken to the streets and ignited a large-scale demonstration that eventually drew hundreds of protesters and truckloads of security forces into a firefight; the sound of gunfire gradually spread until, soon enough, it seemed to be coming from every direction. Judging from the radio chatter he overheard, Naser could tell that the loyalists had been caught off guard. After a few hours, many sounded utterly panicked, unwilling to die for the regime and desperately asking their comrades what to do.

"Leave your car. Go home. Throw away your clothes. Throw away your guns," he recalled them saying. "Eighty percent of the army and police did not want to fight. They hate Qaddafi, they were just stuck." Naser listened as they abandoned their posts.

For those first few hours, things were calm in their area. Then, suddenly, three vehicles came speeding into the neighborhood, trying to escape an attack from another band of fighters. Behind the first two cars was a heavy work truck mounted with a giant machine gun. Nagmi Rayes walked out into the street to get a clear shot; he raised his Kalashnikov and aimed at the lead car, a black BMW 540 sedan barreling toward him from about a hundred yards away. He squeezed off a burst of rounds that punched through the driver's side windshield. The car continued to race toward him, veering only slightly to the right. Fifty yards away, it careened into a wall, killing four of the five men inside.

The city was falling under rebel control, Mohammed Sheikh said later, like a building that collapses in sections. But the very strongest parts had yet to cave, and the cavalry was still nowhere in sight. Those who faced continued resistance were on their own, untrained and outgunned, fighting for their lives.

Elhekti's men felt strong through the first night. Their skirmishes were not too heavy or prolonged. Mansura was bordered by low-lying Al Nasr Street, a main artery the rebels had not yet been able to close off; across the road was the fortress-like state television center, now a loyalist redoubt broadcasting assurances that "all of Tripoli is safe and secure"—despite the sounds of gunfire, explosions, and NATO jets screaming overhead—and showing old video of Qaddafi supporters waving flags in the city square.

Almgairbi and a few others were positioned high above it, on the second floor of the house that Saadi Qaddafi had left empty, shooting down at every vehicle that tried to pass. Almgairbi found himself hauling two or three ammo boxes at a time, when he normally might have strained to lift just one. He believed it was more than mere adrenaline that sustained him. "The enemy knew they were wrong," he recalled later. "We believed in what we were doing. We had our families at our backs."

After they had taken the nearby army post, freeing forty-two prisoners, Elhekti spent several hours circling the neighborhood to make sure the perimeter was secure. He was encouraged by their victory at the post, where troops had quit fighting and scrambled out the back over a wall as soon as a rebel RPG hit the building. But he was worried about technicals, the trucks mounted with heavy machine guns that could race through the streets laying waste to his lighter-armed fighters. If one made it past their perimeter, many of his men would be killed. They had only a twenty-five-year-old medical student to tend to their injured that night, since the doctors they had found to staff their field hospital were still too scared to venture out of their homes.

Around the middle of the night, the loyalists began to try a series of seemingly erratic incursions. Elhekti would hear a shout that a rebel had spotted gunmen moving on foot through one side of the neighborhood, and his men would all run over to fight, only to find their opponents already gone. Then someone else would see fighters in the other direction, and the men would go running back. It was hard to tell what the enemy was doing. Were they probing their defenses? Or just trying to escape? Elhekti realized that he'd underestimated how hard it would be to communicate with his own men. They had only arranged to collect a total of three walkie-talkies among them; Tripoli's cell phone network was still intact, but it was often overwhelmed, and Elhekti didn't have anything close to a Rolodex with all his fighters' phone numbers in it.

A few hours before dawn, he heard the dueling jackhammer sound of a gunfight down the street. He ran over to find three of his allies hunkered down at an intersection, trading fire with fighters in the distance. It was impossible to see how many of them there were. Elhekti just aimed at the muzzle flashes and kept shooting until they stopped. The fighting went on like this for a few hours—intermittent clashes that were decided quickly or not at all, with the enemy seemingly melting away. Elhekti managed to sleep in a few short shifts that night, for maybe two hours total.

The attacks began in earnest around 10 a.m., with waves of fighters trying to storm the neighborhood on foot. The rebels fought pitched battles in the streets as technicals thundered up the main road, orange streams of fire pouring from their guns. Elhekti was cutting back and forth from the street battles to his position at the mosque, getting pinned down at one point by a sniper on an upper floor of a hotel a few hundred meters toward the sea. He marveled that the imam was still full of energy, rushing from one side of the neighborhood to the other, shouting orders and hauling ammunition. Elhekti asked the religious man how he had managed to preserve his strength while fasting. Mshereb replied that, of course, he had been eating all along. "You should eat," Mshereb told him. "We have permission from God."

TOP: *A portrait of Muammar Qaddafi, placed on top of a dead loyalist soldier by rebel fighters.*
BOTTOM: *Rebel soldiers advanced street by street in the final battle for the Libyan city of Sirte.*
All photos by Ayman Oghanna.

A rebel wrecking crew showboats in front of Qaddafi's Tripoli compound,
Bab al Aziziya, moments before tearing the building to the ground.

TOP & BOTTOM: *Graffiti covering the walls of Tripoli's Mansura district, which experienced some of the fiercest fighting to liberate the capital.*

TOP: *Rebel soldiers weep after discovering a missing comrade's dead body in a liberated hospital.*
BOTTOM: *A military parade in the rebel stronghold of Zintan.*

Bab al Aziziya being torn to the ground.

TOP & BOTTOM: *The final rebel assault on Sirte.*

The majority of the main rebel force was still held up in heavy fighting thirty miles away, in Zawiyah. Elhekti's contacts assured him that they would be there soon, but he was not comforted; it sounded like a canned line. What else were they going to tell him—that he was on his own in an all-out war against Qaddafi's army, and that no one could say when help would arrive? He called his friends in other areas, and learned that their chapter of the revolution was already over. Many were throwing parties. Their instructions had been clear: they were supposed to remain in their assigned areas, holding them until the main rebel force arrived with reinforcements and heavy weapons. Elhekti couldn't expect them to come to his aid.

By the afternoon, the fighting had reached a relentless intensity. Qaddafi's security forces had started launching mortars and RPGs, one of which streaked through the mosque's outside wall into the garden but failed to detonate. Several of Elhekti's allies were dead already, and between the waves of fight-or-flight adrenaline he felt hollowed by fatigue.

Almgairbi was stuck on the upper floor of the Qaddafi house, taking cover under fire from the technicals on Al Nasr Street below. At one point, a sniper shot out the eye of the man fighting at his side. Around sunset, they abandoned their position. At the mosque, Elhekti was startled at his friend's appearance: Almgairbi was struggling to catch his breath, his face flushed and streaming with sweat. Since leaving his home the night before, Elhekti had managed to keep his thoughts positive, his mind focused on winning the battle—he knew that the uprising would succeed, and he didn't doubt that the rebels would arrive eventually. But when? He began to fear that he might not live to see their victory.

*   *   *

That night, Nagmi Rayes got a surprise phone call from Dubai. It was an old friend from the military academy— the uncle of Mohammed Qaddafi, the dictator's eldest son. Rayes had met Mohammed several times when he was very young; the boy had since grown up to become chairman of the state telecom company, in which capacity he had pulled the plug on Libya's internet connection at the start of the revolution. He was said to be uninterested in taking over control of Libya if his father stepped down. At the moment, however, he was surrounded by rebels and fearing for his life.

According to Rayes, the uncle asked him to go to Mohammed's home to help negotiate his surrender. It was one of those bizarre moments that take place in a revolution, when the old order sees it has been upended. Rayes told his old friend that he would try to help.

He didn't get very far. Neighborhood fighters had set up roadblocks across much of the city, and Rayes was detained at a checkpoint almost as soon as he left his own neighborhood. He gave the young men his code name, and they called their operations room to verify his identity, but he soon gave up on trying to reach Mohammed Qaddafi. A few hours later, rebels stormed Qaddafi's house while he spoke by phone to Al Jazeera. As the gunshots around him grew louder, he could be heard repeating "There is no god but Allah." Then the line went dead. The head of the NTC soon confirmed he was safe and in rebel hands. The next day, with help from loyalists, he managed to escape.

*   *   *

In the morning, Elhekti's men were still trying to fight off hit-and-run attacks, having moved their ammo stockpile back from the mosque in case they were overrun. But their opponents seemed to be diminishing in numbers, and losing their fighting spirit. It felt like a tipping point had been reached. (Indeed, some rebel forces had reportedly arrived at the outskirts of the city the night before, and the national cell phone network had sent out a mass text message "congratulating the Libyan people for the fall of Muammar Qaddafi and calling on the Libyan people to go into the street to protect public property." In a statement, President Obama declared that "Tripoli is slipping from the grasp of a tyrant... Muammar Qaddafi and his regime need to recognize that their rule has come to an end.") But the fighting continued nonetheless.

Mansura's rebels were still busy repelling loyalist incursions when, sometime around noon, a beige Toyota pickup truck mounted with a 23mm machine gun came speeding up toward their perimeter. Elhekti's men shot out its tires before they realized it was the vanguard of the rebels' main thrust into Tripoli. A local man climbed onto the roof of the vehicle to signal to his allies that it was one of their own.

There was an air of celebration as the women of Mansura came into the streets to greet the rebels, but it proved to be short-lived—within minutes, their reinforcements were gone. Some of the units then entering Tripoli had done a victory lap to boost people's morale, then settled down to camp in schools and abandoned army bases.

Mansura's battle raged on. Rocket-propelled grenades and mortars were still falling on the neighborhood—one came crashing through the roof of the mosque's bathroom—and Elhekti worried about running out of ammo, and about the loyalists regrouping to retake the neighborhood. When he heard that rebels from the Tripoli Brigade—Libyan expats and local men who had left Tripoli to train in the mountains—were setting up camp in a school about two kilometers away, he decided to go and ask for their help. He loaded himself into a car with two friends, and they set off on a long, cumbersome route through the back streets in order to avoid the snipers along the main road. Many of the neighborhoods they traveled through had been locked down with checkpoints, but others were still dangerous.

Elhekti let himself hope that the fighters from the Tripoli Brigade would come back to Mansura with him, but when he arrived at the school, he found them settling in with no plans of leaving. Their commander, Abdel-Hakim Belhaj, was still en route, along with much of his force; according to Elhetki, Belhaj's second-in-command told him that he couldn't spare any men. He was going to wait until morning to attack Qaddafi's compound. Elhekti, crestfallen, knew they would at least have to pass through his neighborhood along the way, so he accepted some ammunition and returned to defend it.

That evening, Elhekti went home for a few minutes to eat with his wife. She had been worried, watching events from their balcony when she could, and asked him to check in more often so she would know he was still alive. Soon thereafter, Elhekti got a call from a friend who lived near the city's central square. There had been reports of loyalists clashing there with the newly arrived rebels, who had been parading around with the tricolor flag and shooting at the square's large Qaddafi poster. Elhekti's friend asked him to come help them fight. It struck him as ironic; for nearly forty-eight hours, he'd been fighting to secure his own neighborhood, waiting for the cavalry to arrive. Now, having shown up, the cavalry had gone and picked a fight in Green Square, and Elhekti was being asked to abandon his area in order to defend them. He declined.

By the next day, nearly three days after Zero Hour, only a handful of neighborhoods were still fighting, mostly around the infamous Abu Salim prison and bases where the loyalists were concentrated. The rebels flocked to the remaining pockets of resistance, finally approaching Mansura. The loyalists fell back in response, and Elhekti stayed in place to distribute ammunition to the new arrivals.

Almgairbi ultimately joined the fight at Bab al Aziziya. As he advanced alongside groups of men he'd never met, pushing deeper and deeper into Qaddafi's stronghold, a complex wave of emotions washed over him. He felt overjoyed that they were winning, but with that recognition came a new kind of fear about the future. The last three days of fighting had been a terrifying vision of a country at war with itself. Qaddafi's Libya had been a place where no durable civil institution, no alternate center of power or national identity, had been allowed to take root; the dictator had spent forty-two years shaping the mentality of the Libyan people, working to keep them obedient and uneducated. Almgairbi worried that those labors had paid off. It was one thing to remove Qaddafi; now it began to dawn on Almgairbi that the work to undo Qaddafi's legacy would be much more difficult than the effort to unseat the man himself.

*   *   *

In the weeks that followed, the newly renamed Martyr's Square exploded in celebration. Young men led the crowds in triumphant choruses of the pre-Qaddafi national anthem. There were popcorn vendors and midway rides and long, panic-inducing peals of celebratory gunfire. In the park around the square, teenagers and twentysomethings gathered around parked cars, bumped American rap music, smoked hash, and drank black-market liquor. Freedom came in many forms.

It was easy to get swept up in the moment, the sense of triumph of good over evil. That was the dominant narrative of the Libyan revolution, at the time: the world had come to the aid of a heroic people to end the reign of a tyrant. But the reality, of course, was more complicated. On my way into Tripoli, my driver, Ahmed, a young man who told me his father had been ambassador to Cuba and was now working as a police officer, warned me that the situation could easily slip into chaos. In front of us was a truck with an anti-aircraft gun mounted on the back, manned by a rebel with a maniacally childish grin. He was swirling the thing in circles, as if laying waste to all the third-floor apartments around us.

"Too many weapons around here," Ahmed said. "Not enough education." He predicted the country would be Somalia in a few months.

Rebel leaders and their international backers were reportedly scrambling to come up with a post-conflict plan. Much of Libya's wealth remained frozen abroad, and the foreign investment needed to kickstart its economy was still imperiled by the throngs of armed, jobless men in the streets. Meanwhile, the Tuareg fighters who had defended the regime were streaming out of Libya with as much of

Qaddafi's extensive arsenal as they could carry, and would soon band together with jihadists to seize a huge swath of Mali.

Sometimes it sounded like the whole city was shooting. It got so you could tell the news by it. Any change in the status quo would prompt gunfire—it was a quicker signal, if not more reliable, than the BBC. You'd hear the clambering of machine guns start up and you knew that in half an hour the newswires would follow with the story: *Bani Walid is about to fall; the rebels suffer heavy losses at Bani Walid; Bani Walid is about to fall again.*

One day, walking toward the Radisson Hotel, where the transitional government's chair was due to arrive, I came across a protest moving down the street—people chanting and holding homemade posters with slogans like YOUR BULLETS SAVED US, YOUR CELEBRATION IS KILLING US. People had begun taping to their shops and car windows a flyer with a photo of a crying infant covering his ears. I spoke with a young woman who was there because her friend's six-year-old brother had just been killed by stray fire. They had formed a nongovernmental organization to raise awareness. It was Libya's first real NGO, she said.

Nagmi Rayes was meeting every day with a group of about seventy people trying to chart a way through the hurdles of post-revolutionary Tripoli. Rayes wanted the outside factions to withdraw from the capital, to stop firing their guns and creating trouble; he said his group was working to convince the army and police to come back to work and take over local security. But the police were nervous, because they didn't have machine guns. The bands of well-armed young fighters cruising the strip in front of Martyr's Square would never listen to them.

The big fear was that the various militias now in the streets of Tripoli would be reluctant to give up power, and that regional and tribal divisions would flare up. One young man, Ayoub Almadani, told me that Ramadan had been a fortuitous moment for the city's liberation, because no one had been drinking alcohol. But he worried it was only a matter of time before the young guys manning checkpoints all over Tripoli would start stepping on one another's toes.

Almadani, who had been working with the new rebel government's Libya Stabilization Team, told me the situation was similar at the top. He believed the lines dividing competing factions within the nascent government were deep and troubling: the recent assassination of the rebel army's top commander, General Fatah Younis, was just the tip of the iceberg. Almadani saw the NTC as a group of expats without much connection to Libya, or as Benghazians, at best, who did not have much support in the capital. It was an indicator of the challenge ahead.

Driving through Martyr's Square a month later, an orange-violet sunset glowing behind the palm-tree-lined corniche just outside his window, Nagmi Rayes nodded to a line of vehicles packed with joyriding rebels firing into the sky. "Still too many of these guys around," he told me. But Qaddafi remained at large, and there were still armed groups of loyalists to worry about. Days earlier, I had been talking with the imam at Elhekti's mosque when the sound of heavy fighting nearby grew disconcertingly loud; Mshereb had had to excuse himself to go help his fighters put down a loyalist uprising.

Nagmi was ready to let the police handle such threats.

"They did their job," he said of the rebels. "We are very grateful. But it's time for them to go home."

His other fear was that Islamists might hijack the revolution. He was particularly concerned about the growing influence of Qatar, and of a Libyan cleric named Ali Sallabi who had helped secure Qatari arms for the rebels.

"He's a fanatic," Rayes said. "They want us like Afghanistan." In response, his thoughts turned in the direction so many Libyans did when confronting the possibility of a different future than the one they had fought for.

"We will make another revolution," he told me. "We still have guns."

For the most part, though, Nagmi remained optimistic. As we turned onto a coastal highway, we passed a small trash-strewn park where parents had brought their children to play. "You see people coming out," he said. "Life is getting better every day."

His optimism would be tested in the year ahead—by challenges to the central government from the militias, by calls for regional autonomy and attacks on the U.S. and Italian consulates in Benghazi, and by the lack of progress made by an elected leadership he would come to see as dominated by too-hesitant expatriates and too-powerful Islamists. Nagmi himself would narrowly miss winning a seat in congress, but he continued to do what he could to strengthen the army.

"For every country that comes out of a revolution," he would tell me, "it will take time."

In early October, I traveled to Sirte, Qaddafi's hometown, to see the revolution's final front. I rode along with Matt

VanDyke, a tall and lanky thirty-two-year-old from Baltimore, who spent much of the ride cleaning and loading an enormous machine gun. Behind the wheel was VanDyke's friend Nouri, whom he had met while motorbiking across North Africa in 2007. They were headed to meet up with their unit, and planned to join a lineup of gunners who would take turns pulling forward to fire at enemy positions. The center console of their jeep was littered with packages of biscuits, a box of grape juice, a jumble of electronics gear, and extra rounds for the assault rifles in back.

I later saw a photo of VanDyke as he had looked back home: a sort of nerdier Tobey Maguire. But here, with his hair and beard grown out and wearing desert camo fatigues, he looked like a cross between Che Guevara and Jesus. He had just narrowly survived a trip through Afghanistan when Libya's revolution broke out, and within days he was getting frantic calls from friends he'd made in Libya a few years back. They said the regime was disappearing their relatives left and right while the international community stood by and watched. "I'll be there," he told them.

In Libya he filed a few journalistic dispatches for various outlets as cover while he worked in secret as a volunteer scout, filming the locations of loyalist weapons caches for his friends in the rebel army. After Qaddafi forces captured him doing reconnaissance in Brega in March—he was ambushed while riding in a truck mounted with a machine gun, along with three rebels and an RPG—VanDyke spent nearly six months in solitary confinement at Abu Salim prison. The international press covered the details of his capture, as well as his eventual escape from the Tripoli prison in late August, accepting at face value the story he had given his family about going to Libya to work as a journalist. "I didn't tell my mother I was coming over to fight," he said. "She'd worry."

After his escape, he wanted to rejoin the revolution. Relief workers told him he was probably suffering from Stockholm Syndrome, but he felt fine, and soon linked up with a rebel brigade. The Committee to Protect Journalists, which had lobbied for VanDyke's release, would later blast him for giving other would-be captors reason to doubt journalists' neutrality in the future—his deception, they said, was a "reckless and irresponsible act that greatly increases the risk for reporters covering conflict." But the rebels seemed to have accepted him warmly into their ranks.

There was one other American hanging around—a short Hispanic kid from San Diego carrying a sniper rifle who was rumored to be mentally ill. He had approached me to show off the small shrapnel wound in his cheek. "That's from heavy mortars," he said. "So get yourself a good helmet and Kevlar before you go out there. Because you *will* die." When I recounted this to VanDyke, he told me, "I don't even want to be mentioned in the same article as that guy."

After Tripoli, the dominoes had toppled quickly: nearly all the remaining fronts collapsed within days, and a flood of countries recognized the NTC as Libya's legitimate government. The last two pieces, Sirte and Bani Walid, had been wobbling for weeks. Three days earlier, the rebels had launched an all-out offensive on Sirte; now around 80 percent of the city had been pacified. Backed by NATO air strikes, the rebels were pushing through rocket, tank, and sniper fire to squeeze the remaining loyalists, an estimated eight hundred fighters, into submission.

NTC officials had said that the fall of Sirte, whatever

the status of Bani Walid, would mark the war's end. Sirte was located in the middle of the coastal plain where most Libyans lived, at a strategic point along the most convenient routes connecting both halves of the country. Bani Walid was more remote, and built on top of a hill; Nagmi Rayes had told me it might be best to simply lay siege to the city and wait. But the sooner the NTC declared victory, the sooner it could consolidate its authority, and claim the billions in Libyan assets frozen abroad.

Once we'd neared the frontline, Nouri turned onto a main boulevard full of pickup trucks tagged with the graffiti of the various bands of fighters they were carrying to the front. Several blocks ahead, two captured tanks were parked near a car flipped on its side. Turning into the parking lot of what must've been a bank, Nouri stopped beside a row of technicals loaded with tube rockets and large guns. VanDyke climbed out of the buggy.

A moment later we found him talking to a rebel who said he had previously been with the Libyan Islamic Fighting Group. The man had a short beard, wore a ball cap and a blue trench coat, and looked to be around fifty years old. Nouri asked if he was with Al Qaeda. The man laughed, shaking his head. "Kill Qaddafi," he said. "To save Libyans." He explained that he had gone to Algeria in 1989 to get "help" to kill Qaddafi; when he returned, the regime had thrown him into prison.

"Abu Salim," VanDyke said. The man nodded. It was the same prison where VanDyke had spent six months alone in a room with nothing to read, nothing to do but think about where he was and what might happen to him next. This man had spent twelve years there.

It started to rain. We made our way into the bank

lobby, glass from all the shattered windows crunching under our feet. From the other side of the building came the bone-rattling crash of tanks firing at loyalist positions. VanDyke asked if I wanted to see where one of the fighters from his unit had been killed the day before. We climbed over the front desk, stepping on a pile of papers that littered the floor, and followed a trail of blood up a staircase. VanDyke picked up his pace at every landing, nearly leaping across the area by the windows, which were exposed to sniper fire and stray bullets. On the fifth floor there was nothing but a pool of dried blood and a crumpled camouflaged safari hat. Outside, I could see four soldiers taking cover behind a cinder block wall and, beyond them, men running into the city center. The fighters there had begun storming the loyalist positions.

The battle in Sirte, like most of the revolution, was waged by amateurs. Many were quick studies. You could see them calmly laying down covering fire as their comrades raced across stretches of open road. But taken together, the videos of that day I watched later were a montage of fool-hardy young men in action: crowds of rebels massed against a wall, pepped up on Red Bull and adrenaline, shooting cell phone videos as their comrades took turns walking out around the corner to unload a magazine from the hip, or drop to a knee and fire off a rocket; men shooting wildly and dodging friendly fire. In one video, a teenager with a Kalashnikov in one hand and a can of green spray paint in the other races after the fighters, tagging buildings as the rebels took new sections of the city.

*   *   *

Late one October afternoon, scores of Libyans explored the grounds of Bab al Aziziya, the palatial compound where, for forty-two years, Colonel Muammar Qaddafi had clung ruthlessly to power. They drove through its bullet-pocked front gate, passing checkpoints, sentry towers, and a wall lined with concertina wire that bore the graffito inscription *GoD BléSS U.S.A.* They continued past another wall, the skeletal remains of a delivery truck, a third wall, then into the streets of a fortified town within the compound, its blast walls riddled with gunfire and its homes singed black from smoke. Finally, at the inner sanctum, they parked in front of a high-ceilinged, two-story building and got out of their cars.

It was a brisk autumn day, with patches of clouds floating across a blue sky, periodically dimming the golden afternoon light to a cold gray. In the eight weeks since the dictator had abandoned his stronghold, the building had been covered in a rainbow of graffiti and looted by frenzied, jubilant crowds. It had become a sort of playground. A boy with a Libyan flag draped over his shoulders sat behind an anti-aircraft gun in the back of a pickup while a rebel turned a hand crank, lowering the eight-foot barrel to horizontal so the boy's father could snap a photo. Not far away, a mother took a cell phone photo of her daughter, a fashionable young woman wearing a checkered blouse over her blue jeans and a white head scarf with Liz Taylor–style sunglasses. She held both arms out, flashing a double victory sign while a red, green, and black flag rustled in the background. Two little girls held their younger brother's hand and posed for their own photo. An onlooking soldier coached them. "Thuwar," he said. (The Arabic word for revolutionary.) They repeated it aloud. *Click.*

Several vendors had set up shop at the inner building's entrance, selling coffee mugs and tote bags embossed with the flag of a free Libya. Inside, anything interesting had already been smashed or stolen. A few young men paced across the graveled roof or dangled their legs over the edge, looking down at the ash-covered circle of concrete on the lawn where Qaddafi's Bedouin tent had been. Along the roof's edge someone had drawn a caricature of Qaddafi—a hairy-lipped, big-nosed figure with his neck in the grip of a pipe wrench. Beside it was a thought bubble that read: MY PEOPLE LOVE ME. Beneath it was written: FUCK YOU, SUCKER.

Such was the full measure of the man's delusion. Just two months before, the Brother Leader seemed to be in control of his capital, safe behind the walls of an impenetrable fortress. The battle for the city had been expected to be long and bloody. Instead, in a matter of days, the dictator was gone. Though few understood how it had happened, the dominoes continued to topple; now, eight weeks later, as children played in the ruins of his compound, a hard reality was swiftly encroaching on Qaddafi's last redoubts.

In a few days, the last two loyalist holdouts would fall. After NATO bombed a convoy in which he was trying to escape, Qaddafi would be captured in Sirte and meet his end under murky circumstances. A cell phone video would later emerge showing the old man alive, dazed but still painfully conscious. The video, which GlobalPost procured, picks up just moments after Misrata forces discovered Qaddafi hiding beside a drainage pipe, stunned by the blast of a poorly aimed grenade his bodyguard had tossed at the rebels. Qaddafi is taking short, halting steps, dressed in a beige outfit that is streaked with blood along the left side. Gone is the round cap he always wore; the sun reflects off a surprisingly bald pate. A fighter in a brown leather jacket is holding him by the collar, flanked by several men on the right. A crowd quickly draws around him, and the man with the cell phone stumbles as he hurries toward them. He tilts back up in time to catch a man in a gray polo shirt and a short beard hunched over, jamming a bayonet into Qaddafi's anus. A dark, reddish stain appears on the dictator's trousers, and he drops to the ground. As they fall in on him, Qaddafi reaches his right hand across to the left side of his face, trying meekly to protect himself. A crazed voice screams, "Muammar." A man with a pistol in his hand tries to drag the dictator to his feet. He sits up dazed. His scarf and shirt are bright with blood. A flurry of kicks and punches follows, and there is a sickening thud of flesh striking flesh. As his captors yell "Allah Hu Akbar" over and over, a man is heard whooping loudly over the sound of automatic gunfire. The left half of Qaddafi's face is covered in fresh blood. For a moment, he looks confused, like he really never saw this coming. The camera is inches from his face. Someone is yelling, "Misrata, Misrata, Misrata."

At the despot's compound, crowds filed out of the building as the rumble of heavy machinery grew louder. One by one, giant yellow demolition vehicles rolled into the square. The first was a Hyundai 210 LC-7 excavator, driven by a young man in a red T-shirt, who turned the huge claw up front on its knuckle and reared the twenty-four-ton machine nearly vertical onto the heel of its tank tread. He was doing a wheelie. The spectators cheered. After a few minutes of showboating, the machines turned and encircled the building. Two long-necked cranes punctured the walls with enormous bits, and began to jackhammer with a heavy clacking sound, sending loose showers of debris. The excavators raised their claws up high and brought them crashing down on the building, which began to crumble in a slow-motion avalanche of concrete. The crowd was ecstatic—a mass of outstretched arms holding cameras and flashing victory signs. Free at last. You could just hear the cries of Allah Hu Akbar over the sound of the building's collapse.

CONTRIBUTORS

CHARLES BAXTER is the author of five novels and five books of short stories, most recently *Gryphon: New and Selected Stories*. He has written two books on writing, *Burning Down the House* and *The Art of Subtext*, and he recently edited the stories of Sherwood Anderson for the Library of America. He lives in Minneapolis and teaches at the University of Minnesota.

T.C. BOYLE will publish the second volume of his collected stories, *T.C. Boyle Stories II*, in October. "Burning Bright" is one of fourteen new stories in the collection, which contains fifty-eight pieces in all, and includes all the stories written since *T.C. Boyle Stories*, the first volume, appeared in 1998.

NOOR ELASHI received a creative writing MFA from The New School. She works as a writer and the co-founder of SweetGemsNYC, a gluten-free vegan baking company.

DOOGIE HORNER is a comedian, writer, and graphic designer. His writing has appeared in *Wired*, *Fast Company*, and the London *Times*, and he is the author of *Everything Explained Through Flowcharts*.

CATHERINE LACEY's work has appeared in the *Believer*, the *Atlantic*, *52 Stories*, *Brooklyn Magazine*, and elsewhere. She is a founding owner of 3B, a cooperatively run bed-and-breakfast in Downtown Brooklyn. Her first novel is forthcoming from Farrar, Straus & Giroux.

NATHAN C. MARTIN is the editor of *Room 220: New Orleans Book and Literary News*, and the author of the *Wallpaper* City Guide to New Orleans* and *We're Pregnant*, a chapbook. He is at work on a book about Wyoming, his home state.

AVERY MONSEN is the co-author and illustrator of *All My Friends Are Dead*, *K Is for Knifeball*, and *I Feel Relatively Neutral About New York*. On Twitter, he is @averymonsen.

THAO NGUYEN is a San Francisco–based musician and songwriter, and band leader of Thao & The Get Down Stay Down. Her latest album, *We the Common*, was released in February 2013.

LUDMILLA PETRUSHEVSKAYA was born in 1938 in Moscow, where she still lives. She is the author of more than fifteen books, including *There Once Lived a Woman Who Tried to Kill Her Neighbor's Baby: Scary Fairy Tales*, which won a World Fantasy Award. In 2002, she received Russia's Triumph prize for lifetime achievement.

PATRICK SHAFFNER was born in Evansville, Indiana.

RACHEL SOMMERVILLE is an Australian-born licensed California private investigator who specializes in death penalty trials and appeals.

WILLIAM WHEELER has reported from Africa, Europe, South Asia, Haiti, and the Middle East. His reporting in Libya, in collaboration with photojournalist Ayman Oghanna, was supported by a grant from the Pulitzer Center on Crisis Reporting.

ALSO AVAILABLE
FROM M^CSWEENEY'S

REAL MAN ADVENTURES
by T Cooper

Real Man Adventures is Cooper's brash, wildly inventive, and often comic exploration of the paradoxes and pleasures of masculinity. He takes us through his transition into identifying as male, and how he went on to marry his wife and become an adoring stepfather of two children. Alternately bemused and exasperated when he feels compelled to explain all this, Cooper never loses his sense of humor. "Ten Things People Assume I Understand About Women But Actually Don't," reads one chapter title, while another proffers: "Sometimes I Think the Whole of Modern History Can Be Explained by Testosterone."

CITY OF RIVERS
by Zubair Ahmed

The poems in *City of Rivers*—the first full-length collection from twenty-three-year-old wunderkind Zubair Ahmed—are clear and cool as a glass of water. Grounded in his childhood in Bangladesh, Ahmed's spare, evocative poems cast a knowing eye on the wider world, telling us what it's like to be displaced and replaced, relocated and dislocated. His poems are suffused with a graceful, mysterious pathos—and also with joy, humor, and longing. *City of Rivers* is a remarkable and precocious debut.

REFUGEE HOTEL
by Gabriele Stabile & Juliet Linderman

Refugee Hotel is a groundbreaking collection of photography and oral histories that documents the experiences of refugees in the United States. Evocative images are coupled with moving testimonies from men and women who have resettled in the United States from Burundi, Iraq, Burma, Somalia, Bhutan, and Ethiopia. In their narratives, they describe their first days in the U.S., the lives they've left behind, and the communities they have since created. Woven together, these remarkable stories and images are a testament to the complexity and magnitude of the refugee experience.

SONG READER
by Beck Hansen

In the wake of *Modern Guilt* and *The Information*, Beck's latest project comes in an almost-forgotten form—twenty songs existing only as individual pieces of sheet music, never before released or recorded. Complete with full-color, heyday-of-home-play-inspired art for each song and a lavishly produced hardcover carrying case, *Song Reader* is an experiment in what an album can be in the early twenty-first century—an alternative that enlists the listener in the tone of every track, and that's as visually absorbing as a dozen gatefold LPs put together. The songs here are as unfailingly exciting as you'd expect from their author, but if you want to hear "Do We? We Do," or "Don't Act Like Your Heart Isn't Hard," bringing them to life depends on you.

HOT PINK
by Adam Levin

Adam Levin's debut novel *The Instructions* was one of the most buzzed-about books of 2010, a sprawling universe of "death-defying sentences, manic wit, exciting provocations and simple human warmth" (*Rolling Stone*). Now, in the stories of *Hot Pink*, Levin delivers ten smaller worlds, shaken snow-globes of overweight romantics, legless prodigies, quixotic dollmakers, Chicagoland thugs, dirty old men, protective fathers, balloon-laden dumptrucks, and walls that ooze gels. Told with lust and affection, karate and tenderness, slapstickery, ferocity, and heart, *Hot Pink* is the work of a major talent in his sharpest form.

PHARMACIST'S MATE / 8
by Amy Fusselman

Amy Fusselman's first two books, *The Pharmacist's Mate* and *8*, weave surprising beauty out of diverse strands of personal reflection. Half memoir and half philosophical improvisation, each focuses loosely on a relationship with a man in the author's life: *The Pharmacist's Mate* with her recently deceased father, and *8* with "my pedophile" (as Fusselman refers to her childhood assailant). Along the way, Fusselman covers sea shanties and artificial insemination, World War II and AC/DC, alternative healers and monster-truck videos. Fusselman's "wholly original epigrammatic style" (*Vogue*) "makes the world strange again, a place where dying and making life are equally mysterious and miraculous activities" (*Time Out New York*).

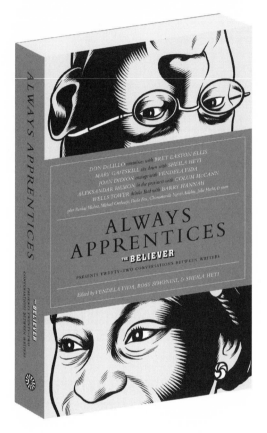

THE BELIEVER IS TURNING

We're celebrating our tenth anniversary with a very special, decennial-sized March/April 2013 issue, featuring:

THREE DIFFERENT FOLD-OUT COVERS

INTERVIEWS WITH JEANETTE WINTERSON, MARTHA PLIMPTON, JOE FRANK, & REVEREND JAMES LAWSON PLUS: CONTRIBUTIONS BY WRITERS FROM MARCH 2003'S ISSUE ONE, INCLUDING SUSAN STRAIGHT, PAUL LA FARGE, AND ED PARK; A NEW COLLABORATION BY RAYMOND PETTIBON AND JONATHAN LETHEM; COMICS AND REVIEWS DEVOTED TO THINGS THAT ARE TEN YEARS OLD; COLUMNS BY NICK HORNBY, DANIEL HANDLER, GREIL MARCUS, AND JACK PENDARVIS; AND MORE!